THROUGH
ADOPTED
EYES

A COLLECTION OF MEMOIRS FROM ADOPTEES

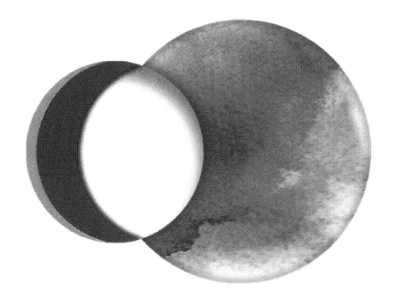

WRITTEN & COMPILED BY
ELENA S HALL

 [Word.robe] Media

2018

First Edition, November 2018

ISBN-13: 978-0-692-16109-8
ISBN-10: 0-692-16109-0

1. Nonfiction - Family & Relationships   2. Nonfiction - Adoption & Fostering   3. Nonfiction - Biography, Autobiography, Personal Memoirs

Published by Wordrobe Media
Printed and distributed through Kindle Direct Publishing.

Cover design by Liz Housewright

Editing and layout by Jonathan Jordan

www.wordrobemedia.com

PRAISE FOR *THROUGH ADOPTED EYES*

"Wow! Elena Hall opened my eyes to the world of adoption through these inspiring and hope-filled stories…It gave me a greater insight into what adoption is like and an even deeper appreciation for its importance and impact on the individual, the family, and society as a whole. If you've ever wanted to know more about adoption, this book is a must-read!"

-Bailey Heard, Speaker and Author,
baileyheard.com, The Ellie Project

"I love this book so much…The personal stories of orphans who have found their forever families are simultaneously beautiful and heart-wrenching."

-Barrett Johnson, *Founder*
Imperfect & Normal Families Only

To My Family

CONTENTS

PART ONE: MY STORY

PART TWO: HELLO, I'M ADOPTED

ACKNOWLEDGEMENTS

In 2016, I started this venture, and I began connecting with adoptees, and I wrote down many of my own thoughts about adoption. Since then, I started graduate school to become a social worker and be an advocate for adoption.

Please know that I wrote this book as an adoptee, not as a student or as a social worker. It was important for me to express thoughts about adoption from strictly an adoptee's perspective. But I pray that my experience as an adoptee will benefit those I connect with on a professional level.

I have continued to connect with adoptees in all walks of life. Some adoptees would suggest seeing an adoption-informed therapist or seeking out birth families, while others would suggest not dwelling on adoption at all. Some are extra thankful for all they have because of adoption.

To you, the reader, thank you for seeking insight through adopted eyes.

To the adoptees featured in this book, thank you for your stories and for sharing a piece of your heart with me.

This book would not have been possible without the following people:

Mama, Papa, Lara, Jonathan, Liz, Hayley, Shannon, Lena, Sarah, Hannah, Brittany, Brice, Rachel, Maggie.

And thank you to Gladney Center for Adoption - my adoption agency in Fort Worth, TX.

Let's Connect! I would love to hear from you!

Email: throughadoptedeyesbook@gmail.com
Instagram: @throughadoptedeyes

FOREWORD

By Jonathan Jordan, Editor

I first met Elena through work in 2017. Our first interaction was when she found out that I am an adoptive dad. "Hey, I'm adopted!" she cheerfully proclaimed. I couldn't have guessed that first interaction would lead to the book you now hold in your hands.

As both a writer and editor, storytelling is a deep passion of mine. Adoption is another passion of mine. It has touched my life in multiple ways. My two older brothers were adopted by our dad, and my son is adopted from Japan. So when Elena told me about this project, I was excited to become involved and help bring it to life.

As an adoptive parent, it wasn't hard to see the value in reading firsthand accounts from adoptees of different backgrounds and perspectives. When we were preparing to adopt our son, we read tons of books by all kinds of experts, but there were few resources from an adoptee's perspective, at least from what we knew of and were exposed to. It seemed - and still seems - like a terrible gap that exists in the learning process, one that we hope this book helps to address.

Adoption has literally changed history when you think of some of the most famous adoptees to ever live: from ancient examples like Moses the Hebrew Prophet, Roman Emperors Marcus Aurelius, Trajan, and Hadrian, and Jesus of Nazareth, to more modern examples like US Presidents Gerald Ford and Bill Clinton, musician John Lennon, and Apple founder Steve Jobs. And yet it remains such a mystery to so many.

Our hope in this book is that it can bring some perspective and clarity to adoption in allowing adoptees to tell their stories. You might not like everything you read in here. You might not agree with everything said. And that's okay.

It was a challenging but rewarding process to help Elena put this passion project of hers together. As you'll soon discover, she is one of the most infectiously positive people you could ever meet, and she stamps that positivity onto everything she does and everyone she meets.

While we certainly can't capture examples of every single possible adoption story out there, she did an incredible job of trying to be inclusive of many different scenarios and situations. Whether you are currently an adoptive parent, considering adoption, an adoptee yourself, or just curious, I think you will find a lot of insight in these pages.

Adoption is a beautiful, challenging, perplexing, and wonderful adventure. It literally rewrites a person's story. It doesn't come without pain and heartbreak, of course, but the same can be said for many of the great things in life.

While I am not an adoptee myself, I am so thankful for the impact of adoption in my own life, and I am honored and humbled that I got to lend a hand in telling the stories contained within these pages. No matter what your family history is like, we can all learn a lot when we take a look *through adopted eyes*.

Jonathan Jordan is an adoptive dad and former foster care worker, in addition to being an award-winning creative writer and founder of Wordrobe Media.

PART ONE:

MY STORY

INTRODUCTION

HELLO...

Hello, my name is Elena, and I'm adopted.

Have you ever thought about adoption? Well, I guess you probably have since you picked up this book. And there is a good chance you know someone affected by adoption. In my experience, people have lots of questions about adoption. Lots. And that's fine - I was adopted and I have a lot of questions, too. In fact, I think about adoption every day.

For example, I really want to know if my love for singing is genetic. Or does that adoration for music come from my parents who raised me around music? Hearing my parents sing, singing in the car, having choir and dance practice every week was normal. Are these things that I am drawn towards influenced by nature or nurture? Would I have liked these things still had I not been raised in my specific family? I love the feeling of hearing the vibrations of my voice and the sound of air leaving my lungs - singing is powerful! Do my birth siblings and birth parents have a love for singing? I wish I knew.

I wish I knew a lot of things. Do we bear any physical resemblance to each other? Do they have blonde hair, too? Are they tall like me? Do they prefer sugary things over savory - because I *know* I love sugary treats. Do they process information the same way I do? I tend to view a lot of things as black and white once I have made up my mind. But I do not know my birth family or how they think.

WORLDS OF GRAY

Our world is not black and white at all. The world of an adoptee is often gray, and the gray is smeared all over the place because of the unknown. Adoptees wonder how much of the world is black and white with all this gray mixed in, and I think every adoptee struggles with this grayness caused by shifting realities.

For me, there are things I know as fact: I have a family. Then *gray* comes in: I also have a birth family that exists somewhere. Adoptees have gray areas in their lives that shouldn't be gray, because, in a perfect world, a family unit would be strong and stay together. It is hard because so much is unknown and we want to make the unknown known. This doesn't mean I want to go search for answers, I just wish I knew automatically. We want to just make the gray known, take away the "what-ifs." I don't mean that gray is an ugly color; I just mean there is more room to process things and turn the grayness into thankfulness for what *is* known.

We all have some gray areas in our lives. What are yours? What are things you wish you knew?

Despite the reality that there will always be gray areas in my life, I think there is hope in clinging to that which I *know* to be true, like the fact that I have a family

So much is unknown and we want to make the unknown known.

who loves me. What is true of all of us, regardless of how much we know or don't know about our histories, is that we are human.

And it is in that humanity that I believe our lives can begin to find hue. Whatever your circumstances, I want to challenge you to turn that gray into light and be thankful for what you do know is true: you are an awesome individual that is full of vibrancy and color.

COLLECTING VOICES

I am not shy, especially about the fact that I was adopted. Different people react in a variety of ways when I tell them about my family. Adoption is so personal, and it is not always a common topic for those whose lives it has not directly impacted. People have questions, which is what led me to start writing. And while I did not have all the answers, I knew I needed to write about adoption, the joy and pain it causes, and the need for people to know more.

I am not pretending to understand everyone's situation. I am not pretending that everything is sunshine and happiness.

But my experiences are not the same as every adoptee out there. I was born in Russia and was adopted at eighteen months old. My adoption is a closed adoption like a lot of international adoptions, and I was never in foster care. My sister Lara was also adopted from Russia, but we are not biological sisters and her experiences have been different than mine. My personal worldview is that of a Christian twenty-four-year-old Russian adoptee with a heart for adoption, people, and ice cream.

My sister and I are not the only adoptees in the world (shocking, right?), so while I knew I wanted to share my perspective, I also wanted to share other adoptees' stories, too. After all, I am not pretending to understand everyone's situation. I am not pretending that everything is sunshine and happiness.

So, I decided to collect more voices for this project, and I took to social media:

> *"Hello All - if you were adopted or someone you know was adopted, I need your help! I would love to talk to you because I am going to write a book or maybe an article...not sure. Surprise! We will just see how big this thing gets so I need your help! Please Private Message me if you would like to be part of this. It is not for an assignment or anything, I just think we have a unique perspective that I want to get out there. Any age/gender/birthplace etc. are welcomed! The only requirement was that you were adopted. If you want to remain anonymous to readers that's an option too! I am going to put together some questions but the writing is to inform people about adoption through our eyes! It has been such a huge part of my life and*

I want to keep sharing that with people. Thank you so much!"

I do not know what it is like to be adopted at an older age, or to be in foster care, or to have a relationship with my birth family, but these circumstances, and others, are *important* perspectives to learn from. As I made connections from my social media post, I sent my fellow adoptees a questionnaire prefaced by the following words:

"First off, thank you so much for your willingness to help me in this project! I cannot wait to see what everyone says! It means a lot that you reached out to offer your help!

Second, we all came from different and unique circumstances so if you hate a question or do not know how to answer it, feel free to skip it - I do not want to force you to talk about something you do not want to. The purpose of the book is to show what adoption means to us and to help people better understand adoption! It would be awesome if people were prompted to adopt after reading these answers!

Tell me the good, bad, funny, and everything in-between! Some of the questions were submitted anonymously online and others were sent to me. Some of them I wrote too. Some of the answers may seem obvious to you, but some people may not know anything about the topic so feel free to type and type and type! Haha! If you do not want to answer questions by writing, I would love to meet with you and go over the questions! Or we can Skype! Whatever y'all want!"

Before I sent everyone the questions, I answered them for myself and wrote down a lot of my personal thoughts. Then I began receiving responses, and it was wonderful to read everyone's answers of hope, heartache, and loss that you too will read by the end of this book. Adoption instantly connects other adoptees to each other, so it is like being part of a secret club that you cannot fully explain.

My hope is that you finish this book knowing more about adoption and the impact it can make, and having at least a glimpse of what the world looks like through adopted eyes. Welcome to a look into the world of adoption.

SNAPSHOTS OF MY LIFE

WHAT IF?

No matter where someone was adopted from or at what age, I imagine it is still a challenge for us all to not play the "what if" game in our mind, like so many adoptees do:

> What if I lived with my birth family and was never even adopted?

> How would my life be different?

I have played this game in my head a lot growing up. I assume I would still be in Russia. My mind trails off into what I would be like: How would I style my hair? Would I have siblings? Would I like the same foods? Would I love to talk and meet people? Most importantly, would I even be a Christian?

The deeper I go into this "what if" game, I start thinking about what role my DNA plays in my interests and actions.

But people always say my mannerisms are similar to my mom's. As you might suspect, the "what ifs" in my life do not really get me anywhere because I can never know the answers.

As I have said, I have always known I was from Russia. This makes the Olympics a fun time for my family because I usually have two winning teams to cheer for! And I like to joke that my parents probably expected to get super-athletic, Olympic-level genetics in their Russian kids – nope, sorry. While my sister is very athletic and likes a challenge, I prefer to sing and dance.

The "what ifs" in my life do not really get me anywhere because I can never know the answers.

My sister and I were raised in the same house, same parents, and yet we are *so* different.

It is interesting to see these differences in the two of us because it makes me wonder what part of it is genetics and what part of it is just the average sociological structure of our family. In our family, I am the older sibling and Lara is the younger, but neither of us held that place of birth order in our birth families.

We do not know much about our past, but I *do* know that neither of us were the first children born to our birth mothers.

Who knows - if I had grown up with older siblings, this may have changed some of my personality.

The "what ifs" in life can go on and on, but unlike other "what if" games, adoption puts these ideas into a bigger realm of possibility because it very well *could* have been my reality. And I don't think the "what if" game is always negative because I think it provides a great opportunity to foster an attitude of thanksgiving!

While I personally think it would be cool to know my birth family, I have a wonderful family now. And while I could have been adopted by a different family, I believe the one I was given is perfect for me!

Some "what ifs" can be fun. For example, I really enjoyed doing an ancestry DNA test that told me geographically where my heritage was. Here was my breakdown from 23andMe:

100% European:
    98.1 Eastern European
    .4 Finnish
    .3 broadly northwestern European
    .6 Balkan
    .5 broad European

For me, it was amazing to know *something*, even if it only reaffirmed what I already knew.

Maybe you play the "what if" game with aspects of your life and think that any of the possible outcomes would be better than your current circumstances. But I think it's important to turn "what if" thoughts into "what if I" thoughts. For example:

"What if I was stronger than stereotypes?"
"What if I am the only positive person someone talks to today?"

And that's yet another way to use the "what if" game for good.

WORDS

If I hear the words "adoption" or "Russia," then I am instantly interested and tend to eavesdrop. Picture a dog whose ears spring up at a familiar sound and you've got a good idea of what I look like.

One time, a couple walked into a store I was working in right around Christmas. It was a baby store full of wonderful clothes and toys with everything you would need to fill a nursery. The couple mentioned that they were excited about the next step in their adoption process when they could finally meet their daughter. They stated that they just needed to get a consulate appointment and then they would get their plane tickets. I couldn't bear just being a bystander and had to know more.

I blurted out, "Where are you going to get your daughter?!" Their precious baby girl was in China waiting for this sweet couple. I was so ecstatic with joy filling my heart that I then told them that I was adopted and gave them my contact information if they ever just needed to talk. The father-to-be gave me a few recommendations about books he had read about adoption from the perspective of the birth parents. It was wonderful.

They asked me how I felt, if I had always known I was adopted, and more. It made me want to rewind life and see my parents getting ready to come get me. I could see the combination of joy and anxious waiting on their faces all while waiting for paperwork to go through to get their child. The thought of it makes me emotional, so on the way home that day, I called my parents and told them I got to share our story again.

It cannot be overstated that support goes a long way in the adoption process. Even as an adult, experiences like this help the bond of adoption grow stronger with my own parents.

CHEERIOS

My mom and dad had been married a few years and then started looking into adoption. Mom called our church who then had a contact for an adoption agency, and when my parents called the agency, one of the first questions they were asked was: "International or domestic?"

My parents saw that Russia was available and then they got a VHS tape of me. The video showed me at different ages with the Russian nurses. At one point in the video, the doctor says, "She was born in

More paperwork, more money... but also more joy.

1994...93..." which still makes me laugh, because, although English is not their language, it would be nice to have a confirmed age. An American doctor later looked at my video and confirmed that I was the age that my birth certificate said and that I was healthy.

I have seen these videos. They were made in the orphan wing of the hospital after my birth parents had signed away their rights. The earliest video my parents received shows me at around six months old. Looking at the pictures of me, my parents thought about adopting me and even sent pictures of me to my grandparents. Thinking about this makes me wonder who else went through this process and did not pick me…

Anyway, it made me realize that any prospective adoptive parents go through a lot, so I appreciate you all. All the money, travel, and emotion. Thank you.

My parents got to Russia, then I was in their arms. My parents' first night with me was in an overnight train ride and they did not sleep at all. It was time for a snack, so they gave me some Cheerios – and it is still one of my favorite snacks! (Cheerios, if you are reading this, I am open to sponsorships.)

Anyway, I just sat with the Cheerio in my mouth, sitting on my tongue, and that was how Mama and Papa realized I hadn't had solid food before. They got off the train and said I was in awe of the cold, the breeze, and the atmosphere. Maybe I had never even been outside in my first eighteen months. While that sounds bad, I do think I was cared for in Russia. I could walk with help at seventeen months, but not alone. But look at me now! I can walk, chew, and everything.

The process of adopting Lara was similar. With me, I was adopted and then they got me. But within a year, the laws in Russia had been updated and so they had to go to Russia, see Lara, and then adopt her there. More paperwork, more money, another passport, but also more joy. I was so thankful that Lara was my sister now. Lara also has her videos and came home to the United States.

Growing up, we knew we were from Russia and we thought that was extraordinary. My parents had always told me that this was pretty special. Ever since I was in preschool, I remember wanting to experience Russia and learn all about this magical *Anastasia* movie-land where I was from.

In ballet class, the teacher would ask where we wanted to fly to. *Flying* meant tip-toeing to the ballet barre with your arms in the air. This was just a simple activity the teacher used to get the children to the barre, but I always told my teacher I was going to Russia. The other kids wanted to go to an amusement park or something, but I was tip-toeing off into much deeper thoughts. My dream was always to go to Russia because I had a deep connection to a heritage and country that I did not know.

LET'S TALK ABOUT. . .

There are other conversations, thoughts, and ideas that are affected by me having been adopted. I remember asking my mom if she had ever had sex. I was probably nine years old at the time.

I had learned that when two people love each other, they get married, and then the mommy's tummy gets a child. (We all know that's not always how it goes, but let me finish telling the story!) Anyway, since my mom never had a baby in her tummy, I remember thinking my parents never had sex. No birth child, no sex. Right?

To my third-grade self, pregnancy was the sole purpose of sex. And since I knew my mom got me from Russia, and there was a plane ride and some money and lots of documents, it seemed kind of unnecessary. When I brought this up, my mom said, "Oh, well, that is for married people, and we love you..." That was a good enough answer for me, which probably relieved my poor mama!

WORTH

My parents have always been so supportive and loving, especially when it came to any extracurricular activities. I loved dance class, Girl Scouts, soccer, and there was also a quick attempt at softball that was *not* in my skill set.

There was one particular activity in Girl Scouts I recall where the point of the lesson was that we are all precious and priceless! It seems like a simple and caring topic. We were asked, "How much do you think you are worth?" My fellow elementary friends shot up their hand in the air with such energy, excited to have their name called on:

"One million dollars!" was shouted out.

"A quad-thousand-hundred...billion...one hundred zillion!"

(Little children are not the best at numbers when it comes to how much something costs or people's ages.)

Then it was my turn. The leader called on me and I said, "Ten thousand dollars!" I was so proud of the answer I gave, because I thought it was the smartest and best answer! My face was probably obnoxiously beaming now with childlike pride because I thought I knew how much I was worth. I knew what my parents had paid to get me! Surely no one else knew how much their parents had paid to bring them into their world... Heck! The other kids were practically free, right? But I had this answer and I was so excited and confident.

The leader looked at me and asked why I had chosen a relatively low amount compared to the other

The other kids were practically free, right?

children that had just said one million. I was so confused because I was so confident, but it was a good lesson in humility. I answered and said that amount was really how much my parents paid to get me.

At this point, this poor leader was probably super-confused, so she asked some more questions and I told her I was adopted. She told me that it was good that my parents got me, but that the point of this was that we are all priceless! Little me really took that lesson literally.

UNASHAMED

Another most embarrassing early childhood moment involves a trip to good ol' Branson, Missouri. The town slaps you in the face with billboards of shows and attractions and Southern hospitality. It's like Vegas, except with family-friendly stuff. Would recommend.

Anyway, at one of the shows, the host asked where people were from. I was six years old and yelled out "RUSSIA!" The audience clapped and the host then tells my parents how thankful he was that we traveled *thousands* of miles to see their show.

My parents corrected this and said that my sister and I were adopted from Russia, which prompted yet another wave of roaring applause and another comment from the host. I was so embarrassed - but I was just answering his questions! I was sad that I had answered incorrectly and I had brought a lot of attention to my parents.

Should have just said, "Texas."

SCHOOL PROJECTS

A girl once told me she thought I was cooler after she learned I was adopted. I did not know what to think of that comment. And it still surprises me that some people do not believe me at all. Why would I lie about being adopted? While there is not a racial difference between me and my family, I do not really look like my parents. You surely have seen those families that all have the same eyes or same smile and you can just tell that their child is a spitting image of the mother and father. Like, they are all little clones of each other. Maybe I just described your family.

Perhaps people say I look like my family because I have some of my mom's mannerisms or I have blue eyes like my dad. It is so interesting to see the "family resemblances" in families brought together by adoption. If the child was raised by their adoptive parents from a young age, they are more likely to be influenced by the parent's actions, mannerisms, and language. But all children also have their own personalities and DNA that form their unique person.

Thinking about all of this is something that would usually distract me from science or sociology lessons in school. I would think about how my family's structure does not rely on genetics. When I was in junior high, there was a family tree project about who our ancestors were. It was exciting to learn that both of my grandfathers on both my parents' sides each happened to own a grocery store!

It was remarkable to research the history of me and my family. The bottom of the family tree poster had my name and the word *adopted* under it. I did not take this as a sign of weakness or a reason to be embarrassed. Instead, seeing *adopted* was special and empowering to me because I was reminded yet again of how awesome it was to have my family.

A girl once told me she thought I was cooler after she learned I was adopted. I did not know what to think of that comment.

In high school, I had another family project. This time, it was to make a DNA chart about physical characteristics you inherit, and I remember that my chart was obviously not scientifically accurate. I told my teacher I was adopted, so I had to remake a chart to hypothesize what my biological family's traits were.

I did not like thinking about it.

I had thought about who my birth parents were, of course, but for this project I kept my mind on strictly the physical characteristics. I focused less on the birth parents' personalities or dreams or hopes - or else I could have sat the whole class wondering and not getting anywhere. I understand that my teacher wanted us to learn about our inherited traits, but I do not like to spend my time picturing people I will never see. On the plus side, I think I got an A+ on the project because as far as I knew, it was accurate.

Another class offered extra credit if you brought in a copy of your baby footprint that the hospital takes when you are born. I told the teacher I did not have one, to which the teacher replied, "I thought everyone had one of those!" I informed him that Russia does not do baby footprints. I remember thinking I could have printed off a random one from the internet or perhaps even handed over my current footprint to him! "Here you go, sir, I do not have a baby footprint but would you like a current one?"

I ended up with no extra credit...

REAL

High school was pretty great for me. I made some lifelong friendships and really enjoyed the organizations and activities I participated in. I was on my school's dance team and every year we had a father-daughter dance. My dad could not dance with me one year, so I needed to find someone else to perform with. We were all sitting in a circle and I asked the group if anyone had a friend or family member that would be able to dance with me. There were a few suggestions made and then I heard:

"Why don't you go to Russia and find your *real* dad?"

As you can imagine, the room became silent. Everyone just gawked at each other waiting to see what would happen next. The only thing I could think of to reply with was, "Good one…" And I got up and left the room.

All this emotion struck me at once. Tears started rolling down my face and my mind attempted to process what just happened. Here I was, a senior in high school, crying because I got my feelings hurt. I had *never* had anyone say anything like that to me before.

Just the idea of my birth family is emotional for me.

And it made me cry because, for all I knew, my so-called "real" dad might be dead. Or, he might be perfectly healthy and happy. Wherever he is, I was probably never going to meet him. So, *no*, I could not just go to Russia and find my "real" dad.

Just the idea of my birth family and going to Russia is emotional for me. It had been my lifelong dream to go to Russia, and it is not a small feat to just get up and go there and then somehow meet a person with my DNA. My head finally stopped spinning and I stood up. A friend found me in the hallway and asked if I was okay. She did not really know what to say, and I am sure the group sitting in the dance studio was still sitting there in awkward silence. I still don't know what was said after I left the room.

I got home from school and told my parents what happened. They were stunned. My mom offered to call the other girl's mom, but I told her she did not need to do that. We were seniors in high school and I could handle it.

To be fair, I really do not think the comment was made in jest or with malicious intent, which is why I tried to not take it personally. I just think she didn't realize the weight of what she was saying. If anything, the comment was made to try to relate my situation to the solution to the problem. For all I know, she might have thought, "Hey, Elena has two dads, let's just go grab the other one."

But for me, it brings up bad memories of abandonment, the reality that meeting my birth family will probably never happen - and, to be honest, I don't even know how I feel about all of that. My dad, my *real* papa, is the one right here who raised me, the one who loved me before he even met me.

THE DMV

Every parent has mounds of crafts, family tree projects, and more from their children over the years. Adoptive parents have piles of crafts and memories too, but they also have a load of paperwork. The amount of paperwork the adoption process creates is incredible. Laws change, government-regulated things seem to go even slower, and everything is documented. This is not a bad thing! I still love to go back and look at all my documents. In college, I was extra motivated to study the Russian language (a course that was *not* easy for me), because I wanted to read all my Russian paperwork for myself.

I have a Texas document that says "Russia" on it, and that confuses people, but it was just part of my US citizenship papers. The most ridiculous thing was when my mom and I went to go get my driver's license. I was so excited, just like any other teen in high school! "I am going to drive! Look out, world, here I come!"

Then we get inside the DMV with all my documents. There was discussion back and forth about my situation, and the lady wanted to see my citizenship papers even though I had a US passport already at this point. She looked at my citizenship paper that has a picture of me from when I was a four-year-old.

She glanced at me, then her eyes darted back to the document. This happened over and over again. I was just standing there excited to become a licensed driver and wondering why she kept looking at me. I thought she was going to make a comment that usually comes up like, "Your parents are so glad they have you..." or, "Wow, that is so special..." Etcetera.

I just kept getting more excited every time she looked at me. I am bubbling with excitement.

Then, next thing I know they had a police officer come stand next to us. *What?* Now I really got nervous, because I did not want to do anything wrong. I said hello and just waited for the next step. I understand this lady was just doing her job, but she turns to me, holding my picture from when I was four years old, and condescendingly says:

"This picture doesn't look like you..."

My mom and I looked at each other, stunned.

I felt the dream of a license slipping away because she had gone through so many documents already with little progress.

"SHE WAS FOUR YEARS OLD!" my mom said insistently.

I froze, thinking I was on a hidden camera show or something.

The lady finally gave me the go-ahead to get my license and still seemed confused why I did not look exactly the way I did when I was a young child. I wonder sometimes if she resembled her four-year-old self.

RETURN TO THE MOTHERLAND

Fast forward to the year 2015, twenty years after I was adopted from Russia, I climb out of a van, my feet hit the pavement, and I am standing in my birth city staring at the building I was born in. I snapped a picture of the building. It was surreal. I have no memories of this place, so it was not a sense of familiarity, but I felt the weight of it all. I was finally in Russia. I had dreamed of this day my whole life and now it was finally here.

I had dreamed of this day my whole life.

Finding my birth family was not the purpose of this trip, nor did I meet them or find out anything about them. The purpose was to make orphans feel loved, appreciated, and laugh. I am forever grateful that I got to go on a mission trip to Russia. It was so amazing and outrageous that I was actually in Russia, hearing the Russian language all around me, seeing the Russian people, eating the Russian food. It was magical.

It was hard to fully focus on my surroundings. I found myself thinking about my life and how I was so close to being just like the kids in the Russian orphanages. Just like the people walking in the streets or riding the metro. What would my career be? What would I be doing right now if I lived here? I had to keep telling myself that this was not my life. I was so grateful to be able to play with the children and see their smiles and learn about their culture that was almost my own.

I expected an uncontrollable catharsis to hit me that day when I stepped out of the van and saw my birthplace. But what happened next was an unexplainable peace. It felt like a hula hoop was around me and shooting out from the circle was a million different colors bursting out into the city around me.

I was calm. I took a picture. Everything was still. Everything had come full circle.

MY TWO CENTS

ADOPTION: noun \ adop·tion \ ə-'däp-shən

People never know quite what to say about adoption. If someone wants to ask me a question about adoption, I welcome the question. However, I will tell someone if their question is not appropriate to ask. Sometimes I brush off a comment because people do not realize the power of their words. They think they know what they are saying but it may imply so much more than they realize.

For example, a woman told me she wanted to adopt, and I was excited to hear this and asked her to tell me more. She went on to say that adoption was a beautiful thing and that one day she wants to get a child and "act like it was mine." Well, now I was confused…

First, if you adopt a child - it *is* yours. It is your child that you are legally responsible for that you should love and care for because it is your child. Second, what part of this is an *act*?

You should not ignore the events that took place before that child became yours because that is part of the child's story! If I was taught to ignore or diminish the first year and a half of my life, that would be crazy. Acknowledging that there are months where I do not know who cared for me and how I developed is part of my story.

No matter what happened next, that time in my life occurred, and it is important to appreciate the events that led to where I am now. Sure, I know what she *meant* when she said "act like it was mine," but so many thoughts rushed into my mind when she made this comment.

It is important to me that you all know how I view and process adoption and give you insight on some of the many thoughts that rush into an adoptee's head when adoption is mentioned. I want to spend the rest of this chapter telling you my personal thoughts and "two cents" on adoption and related topics before delving into the stories of others.

You should not ignore the events that took place before that child became yours because that is part of the child's story!

I know my viewpoint is not the only one that matters, which is why I interviewed so many others with different experiences, but my personal thoughts on adoption are what motivated me to write this book in the first place.

POINT OF SELF-REALIZATION

Every adopted individual has to go through a point of self-realization that what happened to them is sad. Abandonment, shame, feeling unloved… My self-realization moment happened when I was around twelve years old. I realized that it was possible that my birth parents did not want me.

You may be thinking, "But, Elena, was that not obvious growing up?" I know it sounds silly, but I did not actually *feel* the pain of abandonment until the moment I realized my birth parents gave me up willingly. This might be hard for non-adopted people to understand, but ignorance was bliss until this moment.

I knew I had a family that was not blood-related to me, but my parents are so positive and nurturing that I was never curious about the sad parts of my story. I looked at the situation like this: "I did not have a family and now I do." I did *not* look at it as: "My family left me, I got a new one."

While both of these statements may be true, something was emotionally disconnected for me because I had not grieved the fact of my abandonment. While I knew I had a new family, and I grew up knowing I was adopted, my birth family did not seem sad but just seemed like old history in my past. It was normal for my parents to tell me I was adopted and that I was from Russia. I took pride in this and still do.

I care a great deal for my birth family, so I just did not think about them giving me up. The truth is that I do not really know anything about why I was put up for adoption. I *do* know that I had a moment where I was just sad and hurting about the fact that I was abandoned. It is healthy to process emotions and grieve abandonment.

My old orphan life was not even in my conscious memory, but it was a fact that I needed to acknowledge. I was not in denial, but I had always seen the glass half-full. Call it maturing or teen angst, but this time of grieving the sadness in my story helps me better appreciate what my adoption means to me.

It is healthy to process emotions and grieve abandonment.

Grieving looks different for everyone, and while a parent may want to help their child through it, I think that an adopted child needs to realize this reality on their own and process it. The parents can be present to show their love for their child when they need it most.

FAITH

For me, the sadness did not last long. If you ask anyone who knows me, I am a pretty positive person. The tears turned into happy tears when I was again reminded of my faith. Others are encouraged by how the positives outweigh the negatives: a new family, a better life, a brighter future. I will not talk about adoption without mentioning my faith.

I believe that God gave me my family and whether you are a person of faith or not, you can admit that the joy and wonder of having a child and feeling loved is very special. The good truly outweighed the bad.

> [13] For you formed my inmost being.
> You knit me together in my mother's womb.
> [14] I will give thanks to you,
> for I am fearfully and wonderfully made.
> Your works are wonderful.
> My soul knows that very well."
>
> -Psalm 139:13-14 (World English Bible)

I hold the firm belief that the Creator of the Earth knit you together. He made me. He made you. I am comforted in hard times because my faith tells me that I have meaning. There is always a glimmer of joy and hope in times of feeling worthless if I remind myself that I was wonderfully made, because God's craftsmanship is wonderful. I view God as the ultimate loving parent who just wants me to acknowledge him as Father.

KNOCK KNOCK

Have you ever realized how many jokes exist about adoption? You have probably heard, "You're adopted" as the punchline to a joke. You may even be chuckling in your head right now. Now read the punchline through the eyes of someone who was adopted.

Is it still funny?

That same punchline was used in the school yearbook my senior year. I remember flipping through the back of the yearbook and it said a student's name and then, *Surprise, you're adopted!* Someone had actually spent money on that ad in the yearbook to get a few laughs. Not only is this not funny, but it showed that people do not understand the weight of the word *adoption*.

Adoption is a process that can take years - and not just for the parents. Kids can wait years, too. Adoption occurs in many different circumstances, but one thing is the same: it involves a detailed, documented plan, and is never a joke.

I, for one, can't think of anything laughable in knowing that I was put up for adoption by my biological parents. I have the papers that pretty much say, "We release our parental rights." *Ouch*. My heart reads that someone with my DNA did not want (or, at the very least, was not able) to care for me. I do not know the circumstances as to why they signed me away, but it is still hard to read. Everyone wants to be loved. Everyone wants to be appreciated.

It seems like adoptees are either very offended about adoption jokes, or do not care at all. In general, I don't find adoption jokes funny because a lot of them come across as mean-spirited, however I think these jokes I found in *Thought Catalogue* are funny because they were written *by* an adoptee:

- *"My parents like adopting brunette things. Chocolate labs. Black cats. Me."*
- *"Filling out family medical history forms, and just writing in huge letters IRRELEVANT."*
- *"Your parents can't use the 'I brought you into this world and I can take you out' nonsense. You picked me up from the airport, fully clothed with food…"*
- *"My mom loves Chinese Take-Out. How do you think I got to this country?"*

- *"Crafting your family tree in elementary school is like playing a game of 'One of these things is not like the other…'"* [1]

TO PARENTS OF ADOPTEES

An adoptive parent once asked me the following question:

> "The moment when my child is older and starts to really understand their adoption, how can I help ease their grief?"

My parents did not totally notice I had a time of sadness about being abandoned because I responded with positivity fairly quickly. Sure, everyone responds in different ways. The idea that my birth family signed me away is painful and personal. I acknowledged the abandonment, processed it, and moved on. While my parents did not know why we were left, they always said, "We saw you and knew we had to have you."

---

[1] Dietz-Kilen, N. '20 Hilarious Jokes That Only Adopted Kids Will Really Understand.' *Thought Catalog* (2016, June 26) Accessed November 17, 2016.

My personal advice to adoptive parents is to stick with the truth but focus on the story of how your family came together rather than focusing on the abandonment. I think it's good to allow the child to ask you questions and show them their documents if they want to know. You can show them their history since you were not there to experience that part of their life. Be ready when the time comes, because it *will* come.

Your child will figure it out. Let them get to this realization themselves – and help them move through it with your positivity. This positivity can be shown through the adoptive parents always having an attitude of love and empathy with their child on all things adoption-related. There is not a time to tell your child of all the hardships they *might* have experienced in your absence.

A person not talking about their own adoption is not automatically a lack of gratitude.

Once, my sister Lara asked our parents, "Why did my [birth] parents give me up?"

Dad said, "God meant for you to be our daughter."

My sister, being around seven years old at the time, replied, "Oh, okay!" She did not need any other answer at that moment. Kids may just be asking what they see as a *simple* question, so sometimes a simple answer will do.

I think about adoption all the time - if you haven't figured that out already. Whether it's a quick acknowledgment of how blessed I am, or a deep meditation on my life, I am constantly aware of my circumstances.

Just because people are not willing to talk publicly about their adoption does not mean they are not aware or that they haven't processed their emotions. It means they express it in different ways. Just be aware that a person not talking about their own adoption is not automatically a lack of gratitude or realization.

Adoption does not always have a pretty side. Negative adoption stories are plentiful, but one should also not automatically assume the negative. If someone is having a hard time processing their adoption, your responsibility is to be a positive influence in their life.

SILVER LINING

I know life is not perfect and there are very traumatic moments, sadness, and worry. My parents helped me see that I was loved by always talking about adoption positively. I wrote to a fellow adoptee online to see if I could reach out to her adoptee community to find people to interview for this book. Here was her reply:

"Hi. I think you should know that we have many adoptees who did not have a good adoption experience. I'm glad you did, but that doesn't mean everyone else does as well. Have you thought about that fact?"

I wanted to punch the wall! I know full well that life is not all sunshine and rainbows, and I was offended that she thought I, a fellow adoptee, was ignorant to the fact that adoption can be full of heartache. Here was how I replied:

"Thanks for your reply and feedback - I understand not everyone has a positive outlook. Everyone's story has some level of pain and one of the goals of my book is to encourage people to adopt and also help people get a better understanding of adoption so it can be more of a positive experience for everyone in the future.

I want prospective parents to be educated on adoption to help everyone - which may include helping readers know what to do and what not to do. What helped and what didn't. Whoever is willing to share may have a positive outlook, which is great, and most people that volunteer to talk to me do have a positive outlook - but I am open to getting different perspectives to educate readers on different experiences. Thanks again for taking the time to reply and if you do not think I am a good opportunity for your group then I wish you and your group well!

All the best,

Elena"

Be stronger than negativity! You can be a positive influence in your community by advocating for orphans, foster kids, and those that need family. Positivity does not mean ignoring the pain. You can be strong by living a life of thankfulness for your family, or your work family, or your family of friends. Positive relationships can take many forms!

I am a verbal processor. I understand the need to vent and let your feelings out. But when you vent, what kind of reaction do you want?

Support groups feed off of each other. We have all been there, a seemingly simple venting session turns into a full-fledged negativity soirée. Don't even get me started on gossip and how tempting this form of negativity is...

It is unfortunate that, in our culture, people are *affirming* negativity by calling this "support." If someone is venting about something negative that happened, sympathy may come in the form of more negative emotions and negative stories piled onto that in an attempt to relate or be understood. One negative story wants to connect with another and then all we are left with is a lot of negativity.

If there is not a solution, encouragement, or positive empathy combined into this negativity pile, then all a

Positivity does not mean ignoring the pain.

support group is left with is negative toppled onto negative - and negativity is really not what a support group should be using as their stockpile. Even the news likes to add a positive story here or there so that it's not all bad.

If a fellow adoptee is talking to me about their life and trauma they have gone through, I appreciate them talking to me and I try to find commonalities in our stories and just listen to what they are saying. Just listening is a challenge for me because I like to talk, so sometimes verbalizing, "I hear you," can be a good tool! The process of vocalizing a story, especially as an adoptee, is important.

Don't disguise negativity as empathy. Do not act like nothing happened either. Don't ignore the pain, but do not add to the pain by being addicted to negative comments.

Bringing positive language and encouragement into a situation is not denying that there is real pain and trauma.

So, the next time you vent your trauma or share a negative outlook on something, don't get upset if a real *positive* comment is offered. That positive comment is only meant to affirm and encourage you. It is good for people with similar situations to get together, but I think that support groups should always include some kind of practical and positive insight - that silver lining - for members to grasp onto in the difficult times.

THE NICU

My cousin recently had a baby, and I was so excited! When I got to meet my second cousin for the first time, she was just three pounds. She was tiny. She had little hands with miniature fingers wrapped around her mama's big strong index finger. She was perfect. Her mama was whispering words of adoration to her new baby, and simply said, "I cannot imagine loving someone so much."

I was mesmerized by the moment. It was so peaceful. But the moment of perfect silence looking at the new infant was cut short because I couldn't help but think about when I was born. Supposedly, I was two pounds at birth, so it was so strangely special to see my second cousin like this, because it gave me a good idea of how small I might have been. I could not push made-up images out of my head of what my first few days of life were like. And then the thought: how could you leave a little baby?

At that second, I couldn't help but feel a weight of gloom about so many unknowns. Did my birth-mom hold my hand? Did I recognize her voice? What was her pregnancy like? Did my birth parents give me my name? Did they even get to hold me or was I rushed out to get looked at by the nurses?

My cousin looked at me with sentimental eyes, in awe of her baby. I smiled at the baby in front of me while these thoughts stormed through my mind. I began to thank God for the new baby in our family. The storm of thoughts and questions about my own birth swirling around my head stopped.

Many circumstances surround why people are given up for adoption. I would hope that a baby is only given up for adoption because it is in the baby's best interest. I do not know why I was orphaned, but I know that it was an emotional process – it had to have been. How could it not be?

I do not mean this in a negative way - I am so grateful for my life! But these kind of thoughts come into adoptees' minds all the time. We want to know everything about our circumstances, but too often we unfortunately don't have that privilege.

MYSTERY

One of my best friends told me that it was interesting that I have part of my life relatively unaccounted for. This is not the case with all adoptees because they may have been adopted at birth.

I have records of where I was, yes, but my friend is right. I do not know when I first sat up by myself or if I liked to sleep through the night. It does not seem like I missed any big life-changing events, but wouldn't you want to know about the first time you smiled or learned to crawl?

> **It is comforting to believe that my value and worth is not determined by missing time or missing people.**

This aspect of missing time does not bother me too much because it does not change who I am now. It does scare me to think about all the different things that *could* have happened. I could have been adopted by a different family. I could have grown up in a different state or a different country. Maybe I would have been an only child, the youngest child, or maybe one of five siblings. I might have had bad parents. The possibilities are endless really. In fact, I might not have been adopted at all.

I believe that God is all-knowing and He knew what was going to happen. The other ways my life *could* have gone were not really possibilities at all. While this gets into certain theological topics that I find fascinating, I cannot think about the timeline of my life without getting sad and confused but then turning to praise God. Not all people think about God having a plan. Religious or not, it is comforting to believe that my value and worth is not determined by missing time or missing people in my life.

ORPHAN SHOPPING

How could you leave a little baby? I had someone tell me that it was an honor to be adopted and that people who adopt children really are so caring – and I would agree. Then, he said that this was better than the parents who went "orphan shopping." I had never heard this term before. He described it like this:

> *Orphan shopping:* the act of going and picking out a child because one could not have a biological child.

He seemed to communicate that this form of adoption was less of a selfless act to help a needy child and more of a way to just get a little family of their own. That someone who can have biological children choosing to adopt is somehow more selfless than someone adopting because they can't have biological children.

I was not happy about this.

Since then, I have heard similar comments that once you have a family and then you selflessly take in an orphan, it's different than getting an orphan right from the start. Like one is inspired by Sarah McLachlan – look at the needy kids - *cue sad music* - and the other is like some adoption catalogue on TV or something – get 'em while they're fresh out of the oven!

Geez.

It is still a gamble on what kind of person you get no matter if you give birth or adopt.

I guess you could say that my parents were "orphan shopping," or whatever that means. I see nothing wrong with this. Was I not a child who needed a home, too?

- Adoption is adoption. Whatever road led you to adoption, I pray it is still out of the goodness of your heart to love and support the child that is now yours.

- The child still needs a home. You still want a child. The decision to adopt may just come at a different time or circumstance. I understand there are different family dynamics, but the fundamental intention should be the same. The parents should not do it to boost their egos because of the attention it may bring them.

- Sure, people may prefer their child look a certain way, but a child in need is a child in need. Maybe a shopping example assumes the parents pick the perfect flower out of the little orphan bouquet versus an agency presenting you with a single rose. WHO CARES. What matters is that the child has a loving home.

- People worry about the risks you have with a kid that is "unknown." But aren't the characteristics of any child unknown before they are born? It is still a gamble on what kind of person you get no matter if you give birth or adopt.

Maybe one looks more like a hero picking a "charity case" and the other looks like an unconventional way to make a family? I really don't know because I feel pretty freaking proud to have my family, no matter what circumstances brought them to the decision. I'm so confused why people see a difference. I hope you don't see a difference.

Adoption is adoption. It requires love, support, and tons of adjustment. I pray that someone does not adopt so they may look more selfless to the outside world. You are lucky you have the means to get a child, because some people cannot even support themselves. Love your child because you now have a responsibility for them.

So I was put-off by the individual who made the comment about "orphan shopping," because they were unknowingly insulting *my* parents. The fact is that they pursued adoption because they could not have biological kids. But because of the process at the time, my parents actually adopted me in the States *before* even meeting me! If that's not love, I don't know what is.

I heard another person call it "boutique adoption." Just pick out the one you want... This is so frustrating! A prospective adoptive parent gets information on a child that needs a home because it is practical. How else should they do it? Draw a name out of a hat?! But with information, they are able to dream of holding that child. They are able to put a

48

face to a name. My parents did not view this as a catalogue. Yes, I was *picked*, but I was also given up.

Maybe the reference to shopping is so offensive to me because, if you were put up for adoption, you already feel like you were in the "throwaway pile" at one point. Adoptees should not have to feel like a mutt at a pet shop. No matter when or why or how one was adopted, you pray that they were chosen, loved, and fully accepted into the adoptive family.

I *do* feel like I was perfectly picked for my family. While I wish all adoptees could feel this way, I know that not every adoption story is one of love and

If you were put up for adoption, you already feel like you were in the "throwaway pile" at one point.

some end in bad situations. Some people may have been adopted into harder circumstances, but it helped shape them into the person they're meant to be. My parents have never made me feel unimportant or second-rate – and no person should ever let anyone feel this way either, adopted or otherwise. I am heartbroken when adoptees tell me they feel unwelcome in their homes.

DROP OFF

Recently, I attended a conference and we broke out into smaller groups. One of the leaders who knew me mentioned something about circumstances in his lecture and said, "And you all weren't just dropped off at an adoption agency..." and continued his point that I then completely missed. I ducked my head and doodled for a second. *Were people thinking about me? Did they associate me with this comment? This is so awkward!*

Any kind of reference to adoption can weigh heavy on an adoptee's heart.

I brushed it off as I knew he did not have bad intentions and I refocused. A few minutes after the session ended, the leader came up to me privately and asked if he could speak with me. He told me that he was so sorry, that the example was in poor taste, and that he should have never said it. He apologized and told me he did not mean to offend me. That apology made me feel so much better.

Everyone is different and some people might not have noticed the comment. I appreciated this apology because he wanted to see if I was okay, and he said I should not have ever heard any negative comments or references to adoption. I told him it was not the first time I heard something negative about adoption, and he was surprised this had happened before. I know that people do not make such comments to single me out, or to purposefully offend people, it is just that most people do not fully understand the gravity of the word *adoption* or *orphan*.

Helping people understand what adoption means to adoptees is an important reason I wanted to write this book. It is also important for adoptees to be aware that an adoption comment does not automatically mean offense. But I want people to understand that any kind of reference to adoption can weigh heavy on an adoptee's heart.

INFLUENCE

Who is your hero? I am not talking about a superhero with supernatural powers. But who is a person that has made a positive influence on your life? My Granddad was the most selfless person I have ever known. He loved to ride a bike, he loved the Lord, and he really liked ketchup.

Years ago, my sister and I would play our computer games, and he would laugh and say, "When I was younger, I played radio!" He was amazing.

My sister and I would go on walks around our neighborhood with my Granddad, and one day, it was extra cold outside. To Texans, that means below fifty degrees. Anyway, we were all walking and Granddad slowed down and I kept skipping along. I turned back and he had taken a neighbor's newspaper and brought it up to their front door. Then he came back and walked with us. I thought that was so kind.

We kept walking...until he reached the next house. He repeated this little act of compassion at every house on our walk. Soon, Lara and I started to do it, too. We would make it a game to see who could get the most accurate throw. This was just one thing of many that Granddad did that was extra-compassionate. I could fill a book with how kindhearted and wonderful he was, and while I miss him, I am so thankful to have known him. He lived a life of gratitude and led by example.

You have so much power to put a smile on someone's face.

You might not realize how much you influence people. You have so much power to put a smile on someone's face. I hope someone has been able to bless you like my Granddad blessed my whole family. I have heard stories of people who were adopted and then, as soon as they could leave their adopted family and live on their own, they did so.

If this is you, not in touch with your adopted family, I am sure you have your reasons. I understand feeling like you need to find your identity. That's why I had to see Russia. I had to learn about my heritage. I understand the need to prove to yourself that you are *strong*, that you do *not* need anyone, and that you are going to show all the horrible people who have wronged you that you are fine. But make sure that your search for yourself does not appear as a lack of gratitude for those that have provided for you. You didn't adopt yourself.

Maybe your adopted parents were not worthy of a child. Maybe they hurt you. Perhaps an unkind word from a loved one still stings. Maybe you want to show them you are not a piece of garbage. Maybe you want to show the world that you are not helpless.

I want to encourage you that you are not defined only by the fact that you were adopted. If you did not grow up in a loving home, show the world that you are thriving by being the best influence on others that you can be! You can make positive decisions now that shape how people will remember you.

If you were raised in a loving family who wanted you to live a healthy and good life, then I would recommend thanking them for adopting you. Thank them for giving you a safe place to sleep and for being there for you.

At the end of the day, no family is perfect. I am a firm believer that there are many people in this world that should not be allowed to care for children. I am sorry that pain and trauma exists and that some never get the chance to thrive.

If you were adopted, not only are you incredibly cool, but you are WORTH an immense amount to me. If you are waiting to be adopted, you have VALUE. If you are wanting to adopt, you are showing SELFLESSNESS. If you have no connection to adoption at all yet except your interest, BLESS YOU!

I am so incredibly overwhelmed by joy when I think about all the possible ways to show love to others. You are loved. You have value *because* you are able to influence others. What will you do with that influence?

UNLOCKING ADOPTION

In the Fall of 2016, I first began the process of writing this book and finding adoptees who wanted to be involved. Within the first ten hours of posting on social media, I had over twenty-five people who wanted to contribute and let others read their adoption stories. It was so encouraging to go from an idea in my head to people wanting to come along and be part of this experience.

Most of these connections were complete strangers who had been contacted by mutual friends. I called my family and told them about how excited I was that people were interested in this! Bring on all the adoptees! I was so excited to contact everyone.

I started off by messaging everyone individually who had expressed interest or had interest expressed on their behalf by a friend. I did write all of my own thoughts down about adoption before I read any of the interviews so as not to be influenced by their experiences. Everyone was eager to tell me about their own life stories, and again, I saw how quick adoption can connect adoptees because we know what adoption is like. Some expressed thoughts to me about adoption that they had never told their own family.

The interviews featured in this book are real and were edited for grammar, context, and narrative structure, but no changes to their thoughts, feelings, or ideas. For example, some respondents did not learn English until they were teenagers, so at least some editing of content was necessary here and there. I received consent forms from everyone featured in this book and nothing is said without permission.

However, names have been changed to protect the privacy of the adoptees and their families, especially since some expressed a desire to remain anonymous. Also, unfortunately, not all respondents were included in the book due to both book length and content considerations.

Because of the authenticity of the interviews, please know that some of the topics and thoughts may be hard for some readers to digest. There are stories of triumph and joy, and others who just want to get away from any type of family.

You will "meet" a lot of wonderful people through these memoirs. This process has been thrilling, and I have dedicated a lot of time to this book, so some adoptee interviews have updates about their adoption journey that they sent to me months after they recorded their original answers.

Also, the age that an adoptee says they are is their age when they completed their interview. Adoptees range in age from six years old to individuals in their sixties. (Don't worry, I did not require the six-year-old to answer all of these questions.)

Anyway, my fellow adoptees were not instructed on what to say or how to say it. I did not disclose my personal answers about adoption to adoptees because I did not want to influence their responses. I think it was really healthy for me to write this book and most of the adoptees expressed feeling grateful that they were able to write their own answers to questions because it was a way for them to safely process what adoption means to them. But each one of them spoke from a place of vulnerability in their heart.

Adoptees received the following questions, and if someone did not answer a question, it was omitted from their interview:

- Tell me about yourself!

- What is the best thing about being adopted to you?

- What was the hardest thing for you? And how did you deal with it?

- What was the best thing that your parents said to you that helped you understand your adoption? What do you wish they knew?

- Were you in an orphanage or foster care?

- How old where you when you were adopted?

- How did your birthplace influence your adoption?

- How did the age at which you were adopted influence you?

- Is anyone else in your family adopted?

- Are you open to talking about your adoption with people? Why or why not?

- What do you wish other people could understand about adoption?

- What did you wish you knew that you don't?

- Has anything in your life like religion, career, or hobbies been influenced by the fact that you were adopted?

- I do not like when people say "real family" or "real parents." There is my family and my birth family: do you agree? What do you think of the term "real" and is there certain terminology that you wish people would or wouldn't use?

- Are there any questions that you always get asked about? What questions do you hate? Which ones do you love?

- What do you think about jokes about adoption? (Ex: "You're adopted" as a punch line.)

- What is the worst thing someone has said to you about adoption? What is one of the best things?

- Anything else you want to add about your story or what you want to tell people about what it is like to be adopted?

- Any story you want to share?

Alright…with all the "official" stuff out of the way now, it's time to buckle up. Here is a look into the world of adoption, through adopted eyes.

PART TWO:

HELLO, I'M ADOPTED

ADDISON

My name is Addison, and I'm adopted. I was born in Lake Charles, Louisiana and was adopted right at birth. I am thirty-one, married, and have a beautiful six-year-old daughter. My adoptive parents are Christians, so I grew up in a loving Christian home. Mainly grew up in Albuquerque, New Mexico.

The best thing about being adopted to me is that I was chosen! My adoptive parents *wanted* me! That and knowing my biological mother wanted me to have a better life and grow up with a dad, so that's why she put me up for adoption. The hardest thing is not knowing my medical history or knowing if I have siblings. I want to know if I have siblings.

Due to my adoptive parents' situation, I was the only child, so I do not have any brothers or sisters. I am curious to know what medical issues I should be looking out for or knowing what I am passing on to my kids and what health risks I need to look for.

I was in Middle School when they told me I was adopted, so I was old enough to understand what it meant. They explained the story and the why of how I was adopted right out of the hospital after birth, so my adoptive parents are all I know.

Am I open to talking about my adoption with others? Absolutely!!! Adoption gave my parents a chance to raise a child. I was born to an unwed mom and her boyfriend ran off on her. I was able to live a better life than I would have. That's what I wish other people could understand about adoption: how beneficial it is. Adoptive kids have a chance at a better life.

I just think the term *real parents* is wrong. There are no *real* parents. My adoptive parents *are* real parents, because

One of the best things ever said was my mom and dad saying that they chose me.

they raised me. But I consider my biological mother real since she birthed me and I have her DNA. People ask if I know my biological parents. No one has really said anything bad to me about adoption. One of the best things ever said was my mom and dad saying that they chose me.

What do I think of jokes about adoption? Stupid.

What do I want people to know about adoption? That I love it and that I plan to adopt later in life. There are families out there that cannot conceive naturally and adopting gives them the chance to raise a kid and a family.

ALICIA

My name is Alicia, and I'm adopted. I own my own petsitting business in New Jersey. I'm a crazy dog lady who loves photography. And the best thing about being adopted is getting a second chance at a better life. Being adopted gives you a different outlook on life.

When I was a child, I had some emotional problems. I didn't know how to express myself, so I would burst out with anger and sadness. But over the years, I've learned to control my emotions and handle things in a calmer way. I would have to say the credit goes to my dogs who taught me about love, patience, and beauty in life.

I was in an orphanage but I **Adoption means love.** don't remember any of it, and I was three years old when I was adopted. My mother raised me, always telling me I was adopted. It wasn't hidden, so it made that a positive experience in my life. I think being born in Russia and having the experience to live the American Dream is the best part. I wish I knew more about my birthparents.

I think I was lucky because I was older. To be adopted older than a tiny newborn baby is something special, and I'm the only one adopted in my family. It's always been an open subject in my family and with my friends. It's a positive thing, not negative. It's not a bad thing being adopted. Adoption means love.

Yes, I agree with other adoptees that I don't like the terminology of "real parents." But a lot of people have trouble wording it because they don't want to say it wrong. So, I don't get offended by the phrase. I just correct them to what I believe what they should say. My mom who adopted me is my *mom*. My birth parents are in Russia.

I always get asked if I speak Russian. I know a couple of words but not many. Other people ask if I want to visit Russia one day. Yes, when the time is right. I think, because adoption has been such an open discussion in my life, I don't mind jokes about it.

I'm pretty sarcastic, so not much gets to me. Probably the worst thing someone said to me is, "You probably deserved being put up for adoption." But I've been told many positive things about it, too.

Being adopted is a wonderful thing. I could have had a lonely and depressing life. Instead, I got a chance of a lifetime to live a wonderful life. Adoption creates families and it should always be something available for all children around the world who don't have a family. My mother raised me all by herself. Through the thick and thin, she was there for me. She even wrote and illustrated a children's book about being a single, adoptive parent.

ALLIE

Hello! My name is Allie Marie, and I'm adopted. I am a sophomore at Wright State University studying to be a nurse. I was born in Moscow, Russia in 1997. I was left in a maternity hospital shortly after my birth, and a few months later, I was sent to an orphanage. Two and a half years later, a wonderful American family adopted me.

My life since then has been full of opportunities. Growing up, I traveled to many places with my family as well as with organizations. I hope to continue to travel as I progress through my college years. Upon graduation, I wish to continue my education and become a Nurse Practitioner.

They blindly picked a child from across the world to be their own. I still can't wrap my head around the thought.

The commitment my parents made to exert so much time, money, and energy to bring me home is a humbling thought. Often, I consider how lucky I am to be chosen by the family that I have. They blindly picked a child from across the world to be their own. I still can't wrap my head around the thought. I enjoy sharing my beginnings with people because it fulfills a lot of curiosity in the people that I interact with.

The hardest thing for me about being adopted was some of the questions that I received from other people when I told them my story. When I was younger, it felt like someone was tormenting me when they asked me questions, like, "Don't you want to know who your *real* parents are?" When I was below the age of ten, I was not equipped to tell them that I live with my *real* parents.

For most of my childhood, I never told anybody that I was adopted. At the time, most kids my age did not understand. Some of the kids that did know would pass the information on to the other kids like it was a forbidden secret. It made me so uncomfortable that I decided to not discuss it with anyone. I played along whenever the topic came up. People would ask, "Where were you born?" And the common answer I gave was, "Ohio, the state I grew up in." My best friend in grade school did not know I was adopted until we were freshmen in high school.

My parents were terrific about helping me understand my background. I asked very few questions, so I think I made their job easy. I was never curious about the subject. I suppressed a lot of my thoughts relating to my adoption. The only influence that my birthplace has on my adoption is the ability to retrieve documents. My adoption was closed, therefore I was given very little information about my birth mother.

Since I was adopted at a young age, I do not have memories of the orphanage or Russia. Learning English was not a big challenge since I had plenty of time to assimilate to the new environment before I went to school.

My sister was adopted from Cleveland, Ohio. Her adoption was open, so she was able to get in contact with her birth family. After she turned eighteen, she decided to embark on that opportunity. It has been a wonderful experience for her. Even for me as well.

I'm open to talking about my adoption more so now. It depends on the environment of the situation. I still have lingering effects of the thoughts I carried with me when I was a child. As an adult, most people respond with an, "I'm sorry," when I tell them I was adopted from an orphanage. I do not want people to feel sorry for me.

The only thing I wish I knew is if my birth mother or family is looking for me. I only know my birth mother's name and birth date. The validity of that information alone is questionable. Within the last few years, my adoption has also impacted my outlook on religion.

I always consider myself to be the *real* child of my parents. That word is very ambiguous. I wish people would look past that initial identification. I don't know if another label will improve the concept. Nowadays, I love hearing adoption jokes because I awkwardly announce that I was adopted. It makes people feel very uncomfortable! When people make jokes about it, I don't take it personally. Usually, when I speak up about it at the time, the person becomes apologetic and appears more accepting of my situation.

Worst comment I've had about adoption: "I don't want to adopt because I want my own child." Or, "I don't want to adopt because I don't want to have to tell them when they get older that they were adopted." I understand their thoughts, and I respect their point of view. I've also heard people say that adopting a child, especially internationally, is done to make a statement. People have told me that adopting or "buying" children internationally is used as a status symbol. I cannot rationalize with those people.

The first question I usually get asked is if I wish to return to Russia. Followed by if I want to find my birth family. I also get asked if I know Russian and if I remember anything about the orphanage. I never mind answering people's questions because I know they are genuinely curious. Some people are very fascinated, so it provides an interesting topic of conversation. Most people are fascinated when I tell them I was adopted internationally. It opens up a realm of questions.

AMY

My name is Amy, I'm twenty-nine, and I'm adopted. I am one of seven siblings who have all been adopted. I have two biological kids, and I would love to adopt someday. I have so many siblings: biological and ones from my adoptive family. I love them all.

I still struggle with my identity, knowing where I come from, and why I look how I look. Some of my mental issues are genetic and are heightened by being adopted. I also have issues with feeling like I'm still being abandoned. The hardest thing for me is not having a close relationship with all my siblings. My other biological siblings were adopted out in twos. Myself and a younger biological sibling were singled out. I wish I knew them more.

If you were adopted, that means you were wanted by the people that adopted you.

My parents told me at an early age that I was adopted. They always told me I was meant for them, but that I was born to the wrong parents. They've always told me I was special. I wish they knew what it was like to be adopted. As much as I love them, I almost wish I was genetically theirs. Then that would make it more real.

I have two other siblings that were adopted into my family. They are biologically related to each other. Six of my biological siblings were adopted out. I want to know more about my biological mother and father. Also, how many aunts, uncles, and cousins I have.

But I was in foster care from the moment I was born. And I was two years old when I was adopted. I was so young, adoption is all I ever knew. I have no problems talking about my adoption, although I can get emotional. But I think people need to know about it and how it's an amazing thing. It's not just little babies that need homes. There are older children in foster care and have been for a long time. They're looking to be adopted by forever parents too.

I think a lot of things in my life are influenced by my adoption, mainly my relationships with other people. I get asked a lot if I've ever met my real parents. I hate when people use *real* that way. I prefer the terms *birth family* or *biological*, and then I have my *adoptive* or just *my family* when talking about who I grew up with. One of my favorite questions that people ask me is how many siblings I have because I am one of eleven.

I really don't like it when people say, "You must be adopted," or, "You don't look like your family, so you must be adopted." I take offense because it's not a life I chose. I also feel insecure about telling people sometimes. But one of the worst things that somebody has said about adoption to me is, "Adopted babies weren't wanted."

If you were adopted, that means you *were* wanted by the people that adopted you. I like the following idea that I read in a book one time: God wanted me to look a certain way so he made me born to my biological parents, but I was meant to be with my adopted parents.

My adoption story might be different than other people's because I grew up knowing as long as I can remember that I was adopted. I also grew up with my biological siblings, even though they were adopted by other parents. Our parents made sure that we all spent time together. I am one of eleven siblings and seven of us were adopted out. There are four that still live at home with the biological parents, and I don't speak to them.

I met my biological mother when I was sixteen with my older biological sister, and it wasn't really memorable. She didn't know me. I have run into her a couple times since. I always questioned if she ever loved me. My siblings were given away for abuse and neglect, but one day she told me that she did love me and she remembered being pregnant with me and she regretted she never got to know me…

I try to act like it's normal, but I can't help but feel out of place sometimes with my family. They've never *made* me feel that way, it's just how I feel sometimes.

ANDREA

My name is Andrea, and I'm adopted. I was born in 1996 in St. Petersburg, Russia. I was in Baby Home #13 and adopted by two Americans from the Pittsburgh area on July 4th, 1997.

I think the best thing about being adopted is that it makes me unique and it gives me a great understanding of life. My hardest thing with my adoption was not knowing who I was. My parents weren't given a lot of information on my birth family and weren't sure if what they had was

Just because a kid is getting a better life doesn't mean they're going to get an easy life.

accurate. I struggled a lot with myself. I wanted to know where I came from and why I was given up. But they said what any other parent could say to a baby: "Your parents couldn't give you the life we can."

I was in an orphanage, but I couldn't really identify as a Russian because I was only a year old. No one else in my family is adopted.

I wasn't open to talking about my adoption when I was in high school, but that was when it all hit me the hardest. I am okay talking about it now, though, because I've come to terms with it. It's not all sunshine and rainbows. Just because a kid is getting a better life doesn't mean they're going to get an easy life. There are so many more obstacles to overcome even years after the adoption.

I've played soccer all my life. When I was little I would always say to myself, and only to myself, that if I was good enough, I could play for the US Women's National Soccer Team, and maybe my birth parents would see me and that would make them want to meet me. Now I am playing in college.

I hate using the term *real parents*. I don't have *real* parents. My birth parents lost that term when they left me on the side of a street. And my adoptive parents, no matter how much I would love to give them that title, just aren't blood. Yes, I consider my adoptive parents my parents. I love them both and wouldn't want anybody else, but that's just how it works.

When people joke about adoption, I take it with a grain of salt. I was always raised to be proud to be adopted and that's how I always treated it. Plus, it's always fun to come back to someone with, "What's wrong with being adopted? I am." It's great seeing their shocked and sorry faces. I once had a kid pretend to be adopted from Ireland. When I came along and got so excited, he didn't know what to do, and it took him a month to tell me he actually wasn't adopted. Now we're really good friends.

Someone I was classmates with in middle school said the worst thing. He said that no one could love me because I was adopted. But one of the best things was when one person told me how cool it was and how amazing it makes me. I get asked everything from, "Are you in the mafia?" to, "Would you go back?" I don't mind the questions, just don't be naive to it.

Five years ago, I would say I would love to know who I am. Why was I given up? Who is my birth mother? Do I have siblings? What are they like? Do they know who my birth father is? Do I have a history of my health? But now I have all of those answers.

I found my birth mother and my five other siblings when I was a freshman in college. It was exciting but also very hard. She wasn't exactly warm and welcoming at first and told me how she tried to abort me and ended up leaving me on the side of the street. I got my answers from her and haven't spoken to her since. I just don't feel the need to. But I speak with my siblings almost every week, and I am headed to Ukraine to meet them in person for the first time this April. There are happy endings.

ANYA

My name is Anya, and I'm adopted. My sister and I were adopted from an orphanage in 1997 when I was five and she was seven. My parents gave us a wonderful life, full of opportunities, education, and activities of all kinds. The best thing is having a family that supports me, loves me, and accepts me for who I am. We're a family because we choose to love each other, not just because of genetics.

The hardest part is knowing I have a half-brother in Russia who was adopted by his birth father before our parents adopted us. I always wish I could find him or at least know who he is. My parents were never really open about information, so I don't know enough to reach out and find him, which makes me sad.

My parents always said that they chose to be our family because they loved us and wanted to give us a good life. I wish they knew how hard it was that they didn't share our information, like my birth certificate, or who my birth parents or brother are. Once we were adopted, we would celebrate the adoption, but other than that, it wasn't really discussed.

I have always felt a pull toward all things Russian. Hearing the accent is comforting, eating Russian dishes is comforting. I love my adoptive family, and I love being an American, but I also feel very strong in my being Russian, even though I don't speak the language and was raised in a very American upbringing.

I think being five and knowing I was adopted, having memories of different things makes it much more real than if I had been a baby. There's definitely a part of me that I still feel is missing, only because I do have memories and dreams of things. But five is still young, so sometimes I wonder what is a memory and what is my mind trying to fill in the blanks.

I am open to talking about my adoption with others. I think it's important to talk about. It should never be something that you feel like you have to hide or not talk about. If you're adopted and don't want to talk about it, then obviously that is your prerogative, as we all have different experiences. But you should never be made to feel ashamed for wanting to know your birth family or connect with them if you can find them.

I wish people would understand that just because we want to know about our past and possibly connect with our birth families, it doesn't make our adoptive families any less of our family. I love my parents and they are truly my parents. They are my mom and dad, but my birth parents do still have a place in my heart. I can't just forget about them, and I wish it wouldn't hurt my adoptive parents so much that I want to know information.

What do I wish I knew? Health risks, I think, are important. I wish I knew my brother Max. I marvel at how much I can miss a person that I don't even remember or can't even picture.

I definitely don't like the terminology *real family*. Having been five when I was adopted, I was at the cutoff age of having corrective surgery for my eyes, which were

Just because we want to know about our past and possibly connect with our birth families, it doesn't make our adoptive families any less of our family.

crossed due to a condition called Strabismus. The surgery was successful, but when I get tired, my left eye, due to having weaker muscles, sometimes moves inward or outward depending on what I've been doing…or if I'm stressed. I hate the term *lazy eye*. I just wish people would understand that I'm lucky to have been adopted and have the access to the surgery which corrected my eyes and that, even if they hadn't been corrected, it wouldn't change my personality or intellect or things like that.

People ask me if I know the Russian language, but sadly, not having anyone around to keep at it, we lost it. I get asked if I remember anything, how the orphanage was, etcetera. I don't really hate any questions. I try to be open to answer any questions, because I think it's important to start that dialogue so people understand.

Jokes about adoption? I think there are jokes that are off-color that monopolize on any situation. They don't bother me because they don't affect my life. You can choose to be insulted or choose to not let negativity permeate your life.

The worst thing anyone's said to me about my adoption is, "Your birth parents didn't care enough about you to take care of you…" Even if it's true, it hurts to hear that. But I think one of the best things I have been told is that I'm special and have helped make my parents' and adoptive siblings' lives full and complete.

I think my faith is strong. It has helped me through hard times and helps me understand that, though I had negative things in my early childhood, things happen for a reason, and I pray for my birth family and brother, that they are well and okay.

ARJUN

My name is Arjun, and I'm adopted. I live in India, and I am from a small town named Goalpara. I am studying Engineering in a good college, for which I have to work very hard. My parents are proud of me. And about myself, I like all kinds of sports. If I was not an engineer, I would definitely have become an athlete. I also like playing guitar and traveling to places with my camera, that's one thing that gives me peace. That is a little bit about me.

The best thing about being adopted is a thing to be sad about. Like, the best thing about being adopted is having parents, and I am lucky to have such good parents. When I think about it all, it is also a bad thing, too. I have questions. Where are my birth parents now? Where are my siblings? Are they there or not? And all sorts of questions arise in adoptees' minds.

Giving birth is not the most important part, raising a child is.

The best part about being adopted is making my family proud when I do well in my exams. This gives my parents happiness and makes them feel good about me. If I do well, it is showing society that adoption is not a weird thing...or something to pity.

The hardest thing for me was the people. When I was younger, people didn't treat me the way everyone else was treated. For example, when all my cousins were called upon by my grandmother, I was the only one who wasn't called on. I was left sitting in that dark room alone. I couldn't understand why I wasn't called or why I wasn't treated like the others. My family and community said things out of anger that a kid could not understand.

I live in a small town, so everyone knew I was adopted, and my father is a respected person and many people know him. One of the hardest parts was at school, when I found out about my adoption from another child. Children tried to check to see whether I knew I was adopted or not. Then, one day in the class, the student told my friend that he was *sure* I was adopted. My friend got up out of pity and cried for me. Witnessing all of this, one or two tears might have fallen from my eyes, too. I was twelve years old when I was 100% sure that I was adopted.

The worst part was that the whole town knew I was adopted and they showed pity, and I was probably the last one to find out. I overcame that by crying alone. Crying helps a lot. Kids have questions. Since then, I have always been positive about it all.

The best thing that my parents have said was probably from my mother. My father doesn't speak much. She said, "We are so lucky to have you," with tears in her eyes. And those were the moments I knew that adoption is the best thing in the world. But it is still hard for the adopted child to hear. One of my teachers said, "Giving birth is not the most important part, raising a child is."

I wish they knew who my family is. I wish they understand that, and help me out in this. In India, it is not possible to know your birth parents. It is a sad thing, and I don't want to die without knowing. I wish I knew.

My birthplace influenced a lot. The people around me were always whispering to each other. Now I know they were talking about my adoption and that was what made them treat me differently. But yes, it was fine, even though not at all supportive. It was fine. I won't complain.

I am not sure about my exact age when I was adopted. Maybe a month or two old? I was adopted at very young age. So that didn't have any influence on my adoption. I do wish I remembered something about my birth family. As for whether anyone else in my family is adopted? No, no one.

No, I am not open to talking about my adoption with people. And I don't want to be. Apart from the people who already know about my adoption, I haven't told it to anyone. Here in India, if people knew you were adopted they would first treat you with pity and sorrowful eyes. I don't want that. I want them to treat me as I am. So, I keep it to myself.

I wish people could understand that adoption is not a bad thing. Like, people here think that if a couple couldn't have a child, or they have no option, then they go for adoption. I don't want people to view adoption in that way. I want people to make adoption similar as giving birth to their own child. I want people to respect the parents who go for adoption and not judge them meaninglessly.

I wish I could know about my origin, like where I am from. I want to know my biological parents and my siblings. I don't have any siblings and I am the only child that my parents have. One wish that I have been asking to God for, is to meet my siblings. It is the saddest part of being adopted, not knowing anything about your origin. These feelings just break the heart all the time. You want someone who belongs to your own blood.

ASHTON

Hello Elena,

Here are my questions below. This was a great opportunity for me to put my thoughts into writing. I had a great time answering your questions and hope they are what you are looking for…It is a great thing you are doing and I think many people need to hear about adopting and see the value in it, not just for themselves but for children everywhere.

Thanks again,

-Ashton

My name is Ashton, I am nineteen years old and a sophomore in college, and I'm adopted. I am studying business administration and am a member of the Men's Water Polo and Swim Team. I hope to someday own my own real estate company and start a non-profit organization that encourages adoption worldwide.

When I was younger, I did not really think about the importance of my adoption or how it would influence me as a person. But over the years, I have come to the conclusion that being adopted has a powerful impact with the right mindset. I strongly believe that it has become a large motivator for me with the realization that I have been given a second chance that many don't get.

Being adopted is a huge blessing that can forever change your life. The fact that I was taken out of poverty and with no one to care for me, to now living in one of the best places in the world with a great education and a path to succeed is an absolute miracle and privilege that many don't get.

Growing up, I was often teased about being adopted, and I had uncertainties about where I came from and why I had been put into an orphanage. But as I matured, I was able to set those feelings aside and focus on my future and what I wanted to become. I feel that my biggest asset that has really affected my view on my adoption is perseverance and the ability to set goals for myself. I have always had big dreams as a child. I always was encouraged to "go big" by my family which really motivated me.

What was the best thing my parents said to me to help me understand my adoption? To be honest, the truth. I believe that it is important to be transparent with your adopted child on their heritage and their adoption. I feel that it has been easier knowing my past and being able to talk about it than just finding out later in my life.

Being adopted has a powerful impact with the right mindset.

I was in a Russian orphanage, and I was four and a half years old when I was adopted. I think my age played a smaller role in my development than it did for others who are adopted at a much older age. For me, I wasn't really old enough to remember a lot of what happened in the orphanage or my early childhood. My younger sister is also adopted but she is not my biological sister.

I take pride in where I come from. I think Russia is an amazing country that often gets a bad rap. I have always wanted to go back and visit where I come from. I know a lot already about my past and what happened before I was put in the orphanage. The one thing I really want to do is to go back to the orphanage I was in. I want to go to the town I came from and see my culture.

I am open to talking to people about my adoption because I want people to hear my story and be inspired to take action. I am not ashamed of being adopted and I feel that sharing my story can also help other children who have been adopted to find value in it.

For people that are adopted: I want people to be motivated by their adoption. Whether to help the adoption cause or to live a life and remember where they came from. For people that are considering adopting: I want them to understand the impact that they can have on one's life. I also want them to understand that adopting is an amazing experience. I feel many people don't want to adopt because it is not their biological child, or only want to as the last opportunity if they cannot have a child of their own.

I feel that most of what I do is influenced by my adoption. It really goes back to taking into consideration of how lucky I am to be where I am today. I know it's easy to take it for granted, and I am often reminded of my past and the attitude that I should have.

When I was younger I did not like it when other kids would say "real family" or "real parents" when referring to my biological parents. But as I grew up, I kind of came to the conclusion that a *real* parent or family is what you make of it. I know many parents that are not *real* parents based on the way they treat their kids. A real parent, I believe, is someone that really cares about the upbringing of their child and will do everything they can to make sure their child succeeds.

As I get older, more people ask me about my story or if I want to go back. I know there are a lot of generic questions people ask when it comes to adoption, and I love talking to them about it. I typically try to give them a deeper answer instead of a shallow yes or no. I hope that I can cause them to think about it more. My favorite question people often ask me is if I remember my life before adoption. I cannot honestly say that I have a deep remembrance of where I come from, but I do have some vague memories of Russia.

I honestly don't really care what people say about adoption or when they joke about it. In middle school, kids would make fun of it and joke around. But I feel as I get older and am surrounded with mature people, most are interested in my story and don't really see it as a bad thing or something to joke about.

The worst thing someone said to me was "to go back to where I came from to my whore mother." At the time, it really bothered me, and I was self-conscious about my story. After a while, I got over it and learned to embrace my story and take pride in my heritage.

One of the most inspiring things someone told me that helped me a lot was about the many successful people that had been adopted or been immigrants. I see my story as a tool. I have come to the conclusion that, especially in the business world, it is very easy to forget the people you meet or connect with them. Becoming the best in something or getting great opportunities doesn't always come from *what* you know but *who* you know and the relationships you build. I think that having a story like mine really helps me stand out of the crowd and can really show a lot about me as an individual.

The one thing I would say about being adopted, or to anyone who is struggling with being adopted, is that it is a blessing and a miracle to be given a second opportunity. Many children are not given that chance and often are put into horrible situations. It is important to make the best of what you have and understand the impact you can make on society with your story. Having a story like that is a great opportunity for yourself and for others to share the importance of adoption throughout the community. It might be hard growing up with uncertainty or dealing with people that don't see the value in it. But ultimately, as you get older and talk to people about your history, it becomes enjoyable to see them find interest in it.

BRYNLEE

My name is Brynlee, I am thirty-two, and I am adopted. I live in Dallas, Texas. The best thing about being adopted is knowing that I could have the opportunity to succeed and learn about Christ's love, which I would not have been able to experience if I had been raised by my birth mother. The hardest thing for me was wondering if my parents could love me as much as people who live with their birth parents. I dealt with this by remembering all of the great things my parents have done and being grateful for those things.

The best thing that my parents said to me that helped me understand my adoption was when they explained to me that we are all adopted children of God, and so I was no different than any of my other Christian friends. I wish they knew that it was important to me that I try to have a relationship with my birth mother (even though that didn't work out).

I'm not exactly sure when I was adopted, though I was adopted as a newborn baby. My parents say I was adopted at two days old, but my birth mother said I wasn't adopted until I was six weeks old. I'm not really sure my birthplace influenced my adoption in any obvious way, but I think the way my adoption age influenced me was that I don't remember being adopted, so I always felt like I was a part of my family, because I don't know any different.

Yes, I am open to talking about my adoption because I feel like adoption is such a great alternative to abortion. By talking about adoption, I can let people know how it can be such a blessing for both the parents and the child. If I had not been adopted by my parents, I would not be a Christian. I would not have had the educational opportunities I was afforded by my parents. I also would have grown up in an abusive home afflicted by alcoholism and severe anger. I've never been keen on digging into my past, though I now know both of my birth parents. They were the ones who "found" me, though. I was content with not having questions answered.

While it does not really bother me if people use the term *real parents*, I can understand why someone would be offended by that word because I do think of my

I would never change my life for anything

adoptive parents as my real parents, and do not view my birth parents as parents at all. Joking about someone being adopted is never okay. Just like it is never okay to talk about how someone who is adopted is not really a part of his or her family. I have found that the majority of people who are adopted are so grateful to have been blessed with a wonderful family who loves and cares for them.

Most of the time, people want to know how being adopted has affected me emotionally. Also, because I am an alcoholic, people want to know if I know if anyone in my birth family is an alcoholic as well (which is true…my birth mother is an active alcoholic). The worst thing that someone told me about being adopted was when someone said that I don't have a real family, and my parents will never love me as much as their parents do because they weren't adopted.

The best thing that anyone has told me about being adopted is when my birth mother told me how blessed she was when my parents brought me home, and that I'll never know how much she loves me.

The last thing I will say about being adopted is that, while I don't know any different, I would never change my life for anything. God placed me in my family for a reason. My life has been so blessed because I was raised by two Christian parents who value my success. I would not have been afforded these opportunities if I had been raised by my birth mother.

CARISSA

My name is Carissa, I am a twenty-seven–year-old special education teacher, and I'm adopted. I have a Bachelor's Degree in Special and Elementary Education, and a Master's Degree in Special Populations. I have a wonderful husband who is extremely supportive in all aspects of my life, especially with topics of adoption. He has been there for me finding both of my biological parents. I have a wonderful little Toy Yorkshire Terrier who is my little shadow. My husband and I live in a little town called Wolfsville, Maryland close to friends and family.

The best thing about being adopted is having a family who chose you to be in their family because they had lots of love to give! The hardest thing for me to deal with was feeling as though there was something wrong with me that made my biological parents give me away. I went to years of counseling, adoption camps, and wrote letters in a journal to my birth mother often as a child. None of those things helped. I went through severe depression for most my life.

My parents told me my whole adoption story and I always knew I was adopted. When I was adopted, my parents received a letter talking about my parents which they gave me so that I would have some information about them. I wished that they knew more about my biological parents. They were able to meet my birth mother, but I wish that they had kept some sort of contact information.

I was born in Tampa, Florida, and I was adopted through a private agency at three days old. Other than loving hot weather and being a lover of all marine life, which is not from my birthplace, the physical location did not influence my adoption. I believe that being adopted at such a young age, I never had to go through anything traumatic. I also, obviously, have no memory of any life other than my adopted life. No one in my family besides me is adopted.

For years, I wished that I knew if I had any siblings, who my parents were, if I had any extended family, and any health risks. Mysteries can be scary. I always wanted more siblings and that made me hope that I had some out in the world somewhere.

I HATE when people say "real parents." I quickly correct them to say *biological parents* and *parents*. I haven't encountered any other terminology, however, I find all jokes about adoption offensive. It hurts like any race or religious joke. I especially HATE when people say that they wish that they were adopted. I have stopped talking to people because of the jokes or statements that they have made about this. I have had people say that my parents must not have wanted me, but I have also had people say that my parents must really love me.

I do not believe anything in my personal life has been directly influenced by the fact that I am adopted. My mother is more the reason for my career as a teacher. She advocated for me during all of my schooling because school was hard for me. I used to get asked all the time why my parents did not want me. I also get asked about if I know who my parents are. For years I said, "No," but now I am able to tell them about my biological parents and my siblings!

Being adopted is very hard mentally on a child. I went through lots of pain and nights of crying myself to sleep because I felt as though I did something wrong to be given away. I was adopted into an amazing family who gave me anything a kid could ever want, but I still felt unwanted and unloved by my biological family, which was very hard.

I waited so long to find my biological family members and now I have a great bond with some of my biological family. I also learned that I have a biological half-sister from my birth mother, who is twenty-four years old. I also have a half-sister who is eight years old and a half-brother who is one year old from my biological father.

I used to get asked all the time why my parents did not want me...I felt as though I did something wrong to be given away.

I have a couple stories to share:

One day I was watching a show where a bride picks out her wedding dress in a bridal salon surrounded by family and friends. The woman on the show did not have her mother there with her. After watching that episode, I knew that I wanted to find my birth parents before I got married.

That night, I went onto the internet and searched for a way to find someone by their maiden name. I went onto the first website that came up. I searched for the name I knew for my birth mother with a general age range. The first person that popped up, I took the name and went onto Facebook. I typed into the search box the name that I had found and sent the person a message.

On October 1st, 2011 at 1:15 am, I sent this message:

"Hi my name is Carissa. I know that you don't know me but I am trying to find someone with your maiden name. I hope that you can help me. Thank you very much."

On October 1st, 2011 at 10:16 am, I received this message back:

"Hello, Carissa, I am at a loss for what to say and how to say it (that isn't normal for me). I am sure that I am who you are looking for. I bet that your birthday is Nov. 28, 1989...am I correct in that assumption? If I am correct, I truly look forward to hearing back from you."

That afternoon, I went to my friend's house and opened my computer and began to cry. It was the message I had been waiting for my whole life. My friend began to worry and ask me why I was crying. When I told her, she hugged me and began crying with me. My birth mother and I went on to talk about life, that she loved me, and that she wanted to meet me.

Over the next few days, we planned a weekend for me to fly down to meet her! It was the best weekend ever! I got to meet my birth mother and my biological sister, who, at that point, did not think too fondly of me because she thought, "Who is this girl coming in and stealing my mom?" Now we are very close and very good friends.

On August 9th, 2015 I got the courage to finally search for my birth father. I asked my birth mother for some information. She told me that he didn't know that she was pregnant. This was a total shock to me, because she had told me in person and told my parents that she and my birth father made the decision to give me up for adoption because they could not take care of me. She told me his name, which I already knew, and the town that he was from.

I used this information to go back to Facebook and search the name with the city. I found a man who could have been my birth father. He looked the right age, but I wasn't sure. At 8:19 am on August 10th, 2015, I sent a man a message asking:

> "Hello, I know you don't know me but I was wondering if you ever dated a woman named [my birth mother's name] in 1988-1989."

I got no response.

I was worried he thought I was some creepy person that was messaging him. On August 15th, 2015, I messaged his girlfriend hoping that she would have him talk with me. After many messages back and forth, she confirmed that he was my birth father.

He was very shaken up because he had no idea that he had a daughter other than the one he was raising. He was apologetic and said that he would have taken care of me if he had known. I told him that I had an amazing family and that he did not need to feel bad about anything that had happened. We now have a wonderful relationship, and my husband and I plan on going to visit him in the summer!

I am very open to talking about my adoption with people. It is part of who I am, and I am proud of it, even though it is hard at times because of the questions that I am asked. I wish people were more sensitive about the topic. It is hard to talk about, especially for young people and those who wish to find family. I also wish people knew that it is not a "real family" and your "step-family." My family is who I love, who loves me, and they have taken care of me my whole life.

CARLA

My name is Carla, and I am forty-two years old. I am a single mom. I love music, dance, and the arts. I currently live in Washington.

The best thing about being adopted is understanding unconditional love is my greatest reward. The unknown and lack of closure is the hardest. There's a lot of mystery surrounding everything about my adoption and where I come from and who my true blood family is. My actual blood grandparents may be my grandparents, but they had to go through the full adoption procedure. There are a lot of things I don't know and a lot of confusion.

I was adopted out of a military army base's orphanage in Tacoma. I was three years old, and I remember it was around Christmas time. Being adopted at a young age made the transition a little easier. Kids are resilient, but adoption is scary. It can be scary no matter how great the family is. I'm not exactly sure if anyone else in my family is adopted - there are a lot of secrets.

I am open to talking about my adoption to a certain degree, but again, there's a lot of mystery still involved. Growing up, I moved around a lot. I was told many things about my mother. I was told my actual mother was in prison or not able to see me. By the time I was eleven, there was a rumor that she committed suicide. I later found out she was murdered.

Not knowing really who you are and where you came from is difficult. You have to find who you are by yourself.

I found the man who was listed on my birth certificate. It was the worst experience ever. The man who signed my certificate ended up *not* being my father! He told me he signed it to save my life and my mother's life. He also told me that my son, who was seven at the time, had an evil soul and that he was a bad spirit and that he was just like my birth dad…

I never spoke to him again.

Not knowing really who you are and where you came from is difficult.

I have a hard time with organized religion. I have a strong relationship with my Creator on a personal level, and I am definitely a free spirit. My motto is "free to be me."

What do I think about the term *real parents*? *Real* is a very hard word for me, because most people don't have a clue what that really even means these days. To me, things are never what they seem, real truth is very hard to find, loyalty and honesty are almost extinct in the world we live in.

I dislike adoption kind of jokes. I am a redhead, and I heard all kinds of jokes about that, too. For some reason, when you're adopted *and* a redhead, there's no limit to the jokes! I really hate jokes about adoption, redheads, and "your mama" jokes. Usually the jokes show how dumb people can be.

I think one of the most annoying things that just makes my blood boil is when people try too hard to be empathetic and sympathetic. They always want to tell you they understand what your life is like. People are family when it's convenient to them, and when it's not convenient, they can call it whatever they want. People who know where they came from cannot understand, and I can't expect them to. I just wish that people would stop trying to compare their life to mine.

Once your adoptive parents have passed, life turns into a whole new obstacle course because there are answers you will never have. One of my biggest fears is to date someone I am related to. I know that sounds crazy, but I do not know. I do not want to later find out that that person might be my relative. I could be completely attracted to someone, but the moment I see a familiar characteristic in my partner or one of their family members, things seem to go astray and I find a reason to end it.

I wish there was not so much mystery surrounding my family of origin. But I am thankful for my child. I love my child more than anything in the world, and I am so thankful to have the opportunity to know and feel the true definition of unconditional love.

CHARITY

My name is Charity, and I'm adopted. I'm fifty-one, married for four years, and have two kids. I also have two grandkids from my children and seven grandkids with my husband's kids.

The best thing about being adopted for me is having the adoptive parents that I had. The hardest thing was not knowing who you're biologically related to. For years, I just imagined having the best parents and they just couldn't take care of me. The best thing my parents did for me was to always tell me I was adopted and didn't hide it from me.

I was in Hope Cottage[2] for eight days after birth, then my parents got to take me home. My age helped because I didn't get to know other people - just my parents. My brother is also adopted, but we have different birth parents. I wish I knew more about my birth dad.

I am very open to discussing my adoption because I hope to help people someday. I've already helped my friend and

---

[2] Hope Cottage is a foster care and adoption agency in Dallas, TX.

my brother find their birth parents and it was a good thing for them. I wish other people could understand that adoption is something that is very special and not something to be ashamed to talk about. I love helping people find their relatives because of my adoption.

I personally don't like jokes about adoption. I also do not like it when people refer to my birth mother as *mom*. She's my *birth mother* and my adopted mother is my MOM. I always get asked, "Have you found your birth parents?" I hate it when they ask why she gave me up, because my birth mother was raped.

The worst thing I was ever told (and he feels terrible about it), was when I was a teenager and made my dad really mad. He yelled, "I'm going to take you back where you came from." He was just really mad at me and didn't mean it - but it was hard.

I searched and found my birth mom sixteen or seventeen years ago, and it provided much needed closure for me. She lived a very bad life, and I was even more thankful for the family and life I had. I

It takes a special person to give up a baby to loving parents that can take care of the child better than they can.

got to find out medical things and that was very helpful. When my parents adopted me, they were given a sheet of paper with facts about my birth parents and that was so helpful.

I searched later and found my birth sister and we are friends online. We talk some and it's good to know who she is. It takes a special person to give up a baby to loving parents that can take care of the child better than they can. I'm so thankful I was adopted.

CHRIS

Author's Note: Due to his age, I gave Chris' mother the list of questions, and told her to ask whatever she felt comfortable asking him. He was adopted from Ethiopia.

My name is Chris, and I'm adopted. I am seven years old. I live in Bixby. In Oklahoma.

What is the best thing about being adopted to you?
Being with my family.

What was the hardest thing for you?
It's hard to remember.

What was the best thing that your parents said to you that helped you understand your adoption?

They let me look at pictures of myself when I was a baby.

Were you in an orphanage or foster care?

I was in an orphanage. (He was.)

How old where you when you were adopted?

Maybe one or two. (He was two.)

Is anyone else in your family adopted?

Nope.

Are you open to talking about your adoption with people? Why or why not?

Yeah. I'm glad I was adopted.

What did you wish you knew that you don't?

Nothing.

What do you think about jokes about adoption?

I'm happy about being adopted. Jokes don't bother me.

What do you think of the term "real family"?

This *is* my real family!

ELIANA

My name is Eliana, and I'm adopted. I am twenty-three years old. I was adopted from St. Petersburg when I was one and a half from an orphanage, and my parents and I live in Maryland. I recently graduated from Salisbury University with my Bachelor's in Social Work. I currently work as a psychiatric rehab counselor and am pursuing my Master's in Social Work at Salisbury University's satellite campus.

I am an only child and am incredibly close with my family. We have three dogs who we love - we consider them family. We have a condo at our local beach and love to vacation there throughout the summer. I grew up playing soccer, because my dad played professional soccer. He coached me growing up, and now that I am older, I love to play for fun in co-ed indoor leagues.

I love to stay active. I enjoy hiking, snowboarding, working out, taking walks, and running. I love hanging out with my boyfriend and friends. I enjoy shopping and watching Netflix as well.

The best thing about being adopted is the family I was adopted into. I love my parents and whole family, I fit in, I even look like everyone. I am extremely close with them and they have supported me in everything ever since they adopted me. My parents are my best friends. I also love that I was adopted and can tell people I was born in Russia. A lot of people are curious and I don't mind sharing my story.

The hardest thing was learning about my birth parents. Recently, I found out that my birth mother had passed away from an illness (I still am not sure what), and my birth father was murdered, and I am unsure why or what happened.

I still have an aunt, grandma, and a few cousins my age alive. I am still in the process of eventually speaking with them. It has taken a long time, but I am trying to stay hopeful that one day they will reach out to me. After finding out, I was very confused and just in shock that I even found any information out about my birth parents. It caused me a great amount of anxiety and sadness at the time. I wasn't sure how to process it.

I had millions of questions I wanted answered, but no way to get them with the lack of contact. I talked to my adoptive parents a lot about everything, questions I had. I just was able to open up and vent to them about anything on my mind, which was helpful.

I additionally talk to a therapist to cope and find ways to process all of the information I was given in such a short amount of time. Within a day, I found all that out and was mind-blown. I have been able to deal with it better - I somewhat put it on pause for now, but still am curious and reach out to my friend who has been helping me here and there. Being open and able to talk about feelings has been very helpful.

My parents told me I was adopted when I was little. They explained the process and that my birth parents were younger when they had me and were unable to care for me in the right way to provide me with everything I needed and that's when God sent them over to get me. They kept reminding me that I was safe, they loved me, they waited their entire lives for me. I just wish they knew more about my birth family, my medical history, and even

There are millions of questions you wish you could know. It sometimes can be an emotional rollercoaster.

the relationships between my birth family. I think it would be helpful now to figure out a few answers I don't know yet.

Talking to my parents, they told me since my mom was unable to become pregnant they always have wanted to adopt and chose to adopt from Russia. My mom has been to St. Petersburg for work a few times, and I think she knew from the start that there were tons of children in Russia who could have been adopted, which led them to choose St. Petersburg and follow through with their decision.

Since I was only one and a half, I don't know how much my birthplace influenced me. I really don't remember too much from actually being in Russia. However, I think if I was older, it would have a huge influence on me. To this day, I am an only child, and no one else in the family is adopted.

I am open to sharing about my adoption. At first, when I was younger, I wasn't, because kids are mean in middle school. If they ever heard the word *adopted*, they automatically would say, "Your parents didn't love you," and when I heard jokes or negative comments, I just decided to keep it to myself. I also was very shy growing up, so I never really opened up to people. I did tell my close friends, though.

Once I was in high school, I was very open to talking about my adoption. I was older, more mature, and had a better understanding of it and was happy to share that I was adopted and answer any questions anyone had. Now, at twenty-three, I will usually tell people I am adopted right away if the topic comes up, or if any related topic comes up, I am very open and enjoy talking about it.

A lot of people think it's very interesting and are curious. Especially being in graduate school for social work, we talk about adoption, attachment, etcetera, and I will openly share with the class that I am adopted. I have been searching for my birth family, and each class member asks questions and loves to hear any updates I may have.

Additionally, in the field of social work, a few of my clients are adopted and for me, as their caseworker, it makes it easier to work with them because I can relate to them. However, I do not tell them I am adopted, just because I need to keep professional boundaries with them.

I wish people could understand that it can be confusing and, at times, there are millions of questions you wish you could know. It sometimes can be an emotional rollercoaster, especially searching for your birth family. It can be hard at times as well, because, even being adopted as a baby, you always know you were adopted, so there's this other part of you that comes from a whole different country, and you tend to wonder how you would be if you weren't adopted, what would life be like, etcetera.

Also, I think some people look at adoption as a negative thing, and I would want them to know how awesome it is. Some women are not able to have children and when they adopt, that child fills a gap in their heart and becomes their world. Same can go for the adoptee as well: they may not be in the best environment or situation and an adoptive parent can completely save them and change their lives for the better.

I would like to know what happened to my birth parents. I would like to know what illness my mother passed away from, especially since I don't know any health history. What I would want to know now more than ever is why my father was murdered. Was it drugs? Was he involved in different crimes? I would want to know if I had any siblings also.

My career was influenced by the fact that I'm adopted. I have always loved helping others, and within the field of social work, I can eventually work with adoptions, and I think I would love it. Also, I know those adopted and not adopted can struggle with mental health issues, and I love the mental health field. I currently work in that field, and I myself, as an adopted person, struggle with anxiety, and I love helping others that have various mental illnesses.

I never like when people say, "Oh, your adopted parents aren't your real parents." It's ridiculous. I agree there is a family and *birth* family. My family has given me the world, and I consider them *my* family first. I never like to say, "Oh, my adoptive mom or dad," because to me, they are my parents. They are mom and dad. If I talk about my Russian family, I say, "My birth family in Russia."

I think that, when it comes to those adopted, the term *real* regarding parents should *not* be used. When I was little and told a few best friends I was adopted, they said, "Oh, so are your parents here your real parents?" And I said, "Of course they are, they are *my* parents." I know it was when I was younger, and they didn't know what to say or how to word things, but I don't even like saying, "Yeah, my parents here in America are my real parents." They are my parents, they are my family, my best friends, and main supports.

I always get asked if I remember Russia. I don't mind when people ask but I do say, "No," because I was only one. I can't remember anything from that age. I also get, "Do you know how to speak Russian?" I don't mind that either, but I do not know how to speak it. I would love to learn, though. I guess now that I do know about my birth parents, I do not like when people ask, "So, have you found your birth parents?" because that's then when I have to say, "Yes...but they are deceased," and it makes me sad. I do not mind when people ask if I want to meet my birth family, because yes, I would love to meet my cousins my age someday.

I hate jokes about adoption. They still make me so upset. Like I stated before, kids are mean, so when I heard them joking and making mean comments in middle school, it just hurt me, and that's when I decided I just will keep my adoption to myself so I don't get made fun of. Over time, I became much more open and I am very proud of my adoption, but even a few months ago, I was sitting with my mom showing her the adoption memes and cruel jokes. I started crying, telling her how much they upset me. I don't get why people think it's a joke or something to be mean about.

The worst thing that was said was when I was in middle school. I felt confident to say, "Well, I am adopted," and someone said, "Yeah, well, your parents didn't even love you," and it made me so upset. One of the best things is just my family telling me every day, "I love you, Elly - you're the best thing that's ever happened to us." And the constant love and support from my grandparents and cousins.

Also, those not in my family. I have had numerous friends say, "I am so happy you were adopted, or else I wouldn't have met you. You're my close friend, I love you." I've had my parents' friends tell me, "You are so beautiful, your parents are so lucky to have you." Those comments always make me feel good!

I think this one story is kind of funny. Since I was adopted as a baby and have always lived with my parents here in Maryland, I never thought I had a Russian accent or anything. One day, I was getting a snack with a friend in the summer and the cashier was like, "Where are you from?" I said, "Well, I've always lived here in Maryland, but I was born in Russia!" And then she said, "I knew it! Once I heard you speak, I heard your accent and had to ask!" I grew up speaking English, and that was not the first time a story like that has occurred. It has occurred probably three or four times and always makes me laugh because I don't think I have a Russian accent at all!

Adoption is a beautiful thing and I love my parents and family more than ever. It's amazing. They have given me the best life possible!

ELIZA

Hello! My name is Eliza, I'm adopted, and I am twenty-two years old. I graduated from the University of Oklahoma with a degree in Psychology, Pre-Physician Assistant with a Biology minor. I am currently working as an EMT on the ambulance between education opportunities. I played rugby for three years during university, and I absolutely loved it. I have an astounding girlfriend, soon-to-be fianceé. Together, we have two wonderful fur babies: a mellow Pit Bull Terrier and a mischievous Husky puppy! I also am a child of the Lord. I was in an open adoption when I was six months old from El Paso, Texas.

I consider myself very special to be adopted. It gave me opportunities and experiences that I otherwise would not have been given, in which I am so grateful to my birth parents. I also believe it allows me to connect with fellow adoptees on a level that people who are not adopted do not fully understand. I like that I am able to connect with them and that it allows me to be more open-minded and approachable in another aspect.

During my early teenage years, I selfishly thought that my birth mother did not want me, so she gave me away to someone else so she wouldn't have to deal with me. I struggled with self-worth a lot during those years, however, it took an outside perspective and an open mind for me to finally one day make the connection that what I was thinking wasn't her reasoning. She selflessly gave her child to someone who could care and provide for me better than she could at the time. I am not sure how exactly, but it clicked in my head one day, and it caused me to be appreciative of her selfless act that I would assume would be terribly hard for a mother to make.

I wish other people wouldn't feel bad for me...Everyone's story is different than every other person.

I was very briefly in foster care prior to my adoption. Very briefly: two days. My birth mother was very young when she had me, so I was given to my adoptive parents very quickly. My parents were able to take me home when I was five days old and the adoption was finalized when I was around six months old. I think by being adopted that young, it caused me to feel that my adoptive parents were always my parents; it strengthened the bond we had.

I am a very open person, I don't have much to hide so I have absolutely no problem talking about my adoption with others and explaining things when they have questions.

Sometimes, I wish other people wouldn't feel bad and sorry for me - please don't be sorry. I was given a life I never would have had if I were not adopted. I am happy this way, and I think it makes me somewhat unique. Everyone's story is different than every other person who is adopted. Some people went through hell, and even so, I am not sure if they even would want sympathy.

As much as I enjoy surprises, it would be really handy to know my birth parents' medical history, ha! I used to really want to meet my birth mother since I have not seen her since birth, but over the last couple of years, my desire has diminished. Of course, I am not opposed to the idea and would still meet her and my sister on her side, but it is not a priority in my life anymore.

I don't get upset when people use the term *real family*, but I definitely could see how that term could be offensive. I do have my birth family and my adoptive family, and I understand all the terms can get confusing. Although, I do get a little annoyed when people say "step-family" instead of "adoptive family," yet I understand if they are not familiar with the proper terms.

I absolutely hate when I tell people that my birth parents were teenagers when they had me and gave me up for adoption and their reply is, "Oh, you were an oops baby," or, "You were a mistake." No, I may have been an "oops" or whatever to them since they were not expecting me, but God planned for me to be here and for me to be raised with an infertile couple who wanted children. I was the answer to a prayer they had been praying for, for many years, and I am loved. I was put on this Earth to serve my purpose, one way or another. How comforting it is to know you helped someone else's life with your purpose.

Being adopted is a privilege not experienced by most. I am so incredibly thankful for my birth and adopted families. I know that I definitely would not be the person I am today without them or the opportunities and experiences they have blessed me with, and for that I am forever grateful for their selflessness to give me up and to take on, what my adoptive father called "an eighteen year experiment" that required a lot of love, patience, and money (haha).

EMERY

My name is Emery, and I'm adopted from Lanxi, China. I have a mom, dad, and brother (he was not adopted). I was dropped off at a police station and know nothing about my birth family. I was adopted into a Christian family. If I never was adopted I may never have heard the about Jesus. I very well could have been Buddhist.

I was in an orphanage before I was adopted at nine months old. Since I was just a baby when I was adopted, I always grew up knowing I was adopted. I was loved from such a young age that it never affected me negatively. I wish they knew more details about when I was a baby. China had the one-child policy and boys are the preferred gender. Therefore, it is very common for girls to be adopted from China.

Yes, I'm open to talking about my adoption because it's obvious I was adopted if people have seen pictures of my family. I feel like when I was little I wasn't as open, but now I am. Adoption is an amazing gift. More people should adopt instead of having so many kids because there are a lot of kids out there with no families.

Most of the time, I don't really even notice I'm adopted.

The hardest thing is not knowing anything about my birth family or details of my birth (weight, time of birth, picture of me when I born). I would like to know if I have a brother, who my biological parents are, to confirm the date and time of my birth, and how much I weighed when I was born.

I don't like when people say "real family" or "real parents." Just because my adopted parents are not my biological family doesn't mean they aren't my real parents. I get asked all the time: "Would you want to go back to China? Do you know Chinese?" I don't like when people ask if I know Chinese, because I was only a baby when I lived there. But I would love to go back and visit China someday!

I never really hear any jokes about adoption, doesn't really bother me. I don't think anyone has said something really bad about my adoption.

Most of the time, I don't really even notice I'm adopted. Everyone in my family is white and it's not like I actually see myself when I'm with them, haha! So the best thing is just knowing how much I'm loved by my family, whether I was adopted or not.

EMILY

My name is Emily and people call me Emmy, and I'm adopted from Perm, Russia. I was in an orphanage, and I was six months old at adoption. I have a younger sister who is also adopted from Russia. Right now, I'm going to school in Boston.

The best thing about being adopted is being a part of a family as opposed to being alone. I'm a pretty existential person so it always bothers me that I'm an "accident." I'm nonreligious, so I'm hyper-aware of my original identity as an unwanted child with no family history or defined purpose. I deal with this reality by trying to make something out of my life. I'm pursuing an art-based education and hope to make works of art that'll outlast me.

When I was little, my parents gave me a bunch of books explaining adoption. They also emphasized that being adopted was something to be proud of and not shameful. I wish they knew that storybooks can only go so far, but it's the thought that counts.

Imagine a book chronicling someone's entire life. The first page is missing, but the rest of the book is intact. You can figure out the rest of the book by simply reading from the next page. But don't you want to know what was on that first page?

I don't know much about Perm, Russia except that it is a major city. I do know that Russia does some weird, sketchy stuff to get children adopted quicker, like mess with health records even when a child is healthy. I was really young, so I have no memory of my birth parents. All I've ever known is my Mom and Dad. I would like to know why I was put up for adoption.

I am rather open about my adoption, although I feel at times I am too open. I get so many dumb questions and I make other people feel awkward. I wish people could understand one does not simply *find* their birth parents.

I am an artist. I use my art to compensate for being adopted and feeling worthless. As far as religion goes, I don't think my adoption had an effect on it. I tend to be a rational thinker and I was never a religious person despite going to Catholic school.

I dated this one guy that was trying too hard to empathize with me, and he kept calling my Mom and Dad my "stepmom and stepdad." He explained to me that he had a friend who was adopted and that's what he called his parents, but that person's circumstances were much different than mine. I know it varies from person to person on this issue, but I have known and been raised by my mom and dad all of my life. I don't really like the term *real* parents in reference to my birth parents. They're my birth parents, and Mom and Dad are my real parents.

Imagine a book chronicling someone's entire life. The first page is missing, but the rest of the book is intact.

I've met people who have not only dealt with the adoption process but specifically the Russian/Eastern European adoption process. They know what questions to ask and which ones not to ask. I can tolerate ignorance to a certain point. I of course won't verbalize my disdain, but there's only so many times I can answer, "Do you know Russian?" or, "Will you ever go back to Russia to visit your birth parents?" I'll go back when I'm done with college and my student loans are paid off.

One semester, I was doing a wood shop class. I was in the wood shop with the monitor and a really immature classmate of mine. Somehow, my adoption came up, and the classmate said, "So, you're like from Moscow?" I tried to explain to him that I'm from a different city in Russia. "Well, it's like the same thing as Moscow, right?"

At this point, the monitor chimed in, curious about my adoption. She asked if I knew why I was put up for adoption. I said that I have some theories, but they're pretty dark and I'd much rather them not be true. She said, "Oh, so you think your birth mom got raped?" While that was exactly what I was talking about, I found it very unprofessional from such an otherwise sweet woman. To make matters worse, she blurted that out in front of someone who cannot conceptualize a country having more than one city. I skirted around any further discussion and continued to do my project awkwardly.

I don't hear many adoption jokes, but I'm also not one to get easily offended. My favorite *Cyanide and Happiness* comic is the one where the dad asks his son for "dop-ted." I've been told that I'm better off being in America than in Russia. I know from an economic standpoint that is true, but it undermines any issues with my family, my community, and my country.

My favorite thing to hear when I tell someone that I'm from Russia is any story about Russia that they know. Some people may be from there, some people have relatives there, and some are also adopted from there. Every person I meet that has a tie to Russia adds a piece to the puzzle of my identity.

ERICA

Hello. My American name is Erica, and my birth name was Katya. I was adopted from Ryazansksaya, Russia. I am twenty-one years old, and I now live in New York. Sadly, I found out about my adoption all on my own, I looked in the box full of papers…that were in all English. I was in an orphanage, and I was a fourteen-month-old baby when my parents got me.

The hardest thing about my adoption is that my adopted parents are always joking about my birth mother. It is difficult because it makes me feel like my real parents are in Russia, and I feel more Russian than American. I don't feel American at all. I feel like a puzzle piece is missing in my life. I dream of going to Russia and finding my past.

I love the Russian culture. I also listen to Russian music. I want to learn their language and alphabet. I am very curious to know my past, and Russia holds a very special place in my heart. No one can take that away from me. I have an adopted brother. He does not care about his Russian heritage. I say "adopted mother and father" and "birth mother and father" when talking about my family.

The hardest thing about my adoption is that my adopted parents are always joking about my birth mother.

Absolutely yes, I am open to talking about my adoption, because I love Russia, and I want to go back to Russia. I want people to know that it's okay to ask me questions. I love all questions! It is fine to ask me anything. Also, I want to know my birth family.

But I get mad and I hate when people joke about it, when they don't even care about the subject of adoption. I hate it when people say "you're adopted" in a negative way - like they are totally shocked.

ERIN

Hello, my name is Erin, and I'm adopted. I am twenty-two years old, and my given birth name is Olga. I was in an orphanage, and I was two and a half years old when I was adopted. I currently live in Canada.

The best thing about being adopted is to know you can be loved even if the people you are around are not blood. I always have to remember the choice that my mother made to give me up for adoption was for my own wellbeing. I can never be mad at her for what she chose. The hardest thing for me growing up was not knowing why my birth mother did what she did. Who was my family back in Russia?

To help me deal with that, I would write letters to my birth family and birth mother as if I was going to see her. I always kept the letters for myself to read back through when I was missing her. It helped me feel closer to her even though I was all the way around the world. A couple months ago, I did find my birth family and have been talking to them a little bit, but the translation is hard to understand. We manage.

The best thing my parents have told me about my adoption was that my birth mother chose this life for me because she wasn't able to manage and support me in the way she knew I deserved for my life. I am in a better place, but I know she is still thinking about me. I wish my adoptive parents knew and understood how hard it hurts to just want to have a hug from my birth mom. They can see I am upset when I cry but the actual feeling of being alone and crying for your birth mother to hold you is unreal.

My birth place had a huge influence on my adoption. Russia is a large country and the chances of ever finding my birth parents were slim to none. It is my dream to visit Russia.

The age at which I was adopted didn't influence me much growing up because I was too young to remember anything. I am very glad I was adopted when I was young. I wouldn't have wanted to be adopted when I was in my early adolescent years and remember being an orphan. I think that would be very painful while growing up!

I wish other people who weren't adopted would realize that they don't understand how we feel.

I am the only one in my family who is adopted. My adoptive parents had three other children before they adopted me. I am the youngest. I have two brothers and one sister who aren't blood-related to me.

I am open to talking about my adoption to people because I now have a better understanding of why it happened the way it did. I wish other people who weren't adopted would realize that they don't understand how we feel. They can sympathize for us but to say, "I understand," is so wrong! Also, I take jokes about adoption very seriously and I don't like them.

I wish I knew why my birth mother put me up for adoption and not my birth sisters. Who are my *real* family, my *real* parents? They are both real. They are both my family, just one of them lives in Russia.

If there's one question I get asked a lot about, it would be:

"What age were you when you were adopted and do you remember it?" I wouldn't say I *hate* being asked questions all the time, but when I was younger, I didn't like talking about it because I didn't know much about my adoption. Now, if I get asked the same question, I still feel uncomfortable talking about it, but at least I can answer the question because I know more information.

GINNY

My name is Ginny, and I'm adopted. I am twenty-two, I love makeup, riding horses, and I went to esthetics school. I was adopted from Russia, and I now live in Maryland. The best thing about being adopted is being welcomed into a loving family and given an amazing life. Getting an education and having grown up in a stable environment, I'm so thankful for my parents that raised me. I was ten months old when I was adopted and before that, I was in an orphanage in Novosibirsk, Russia.

The hardest thing I've faced is losing my dad. He was my hero. He held our family together. I was twelve when he died. Growing up without him made it really hard. I often thought about my birth parents and if I had stayed. What would life have been like with them? Was my birth father nice, and would I love him as much as my dad? When he (my dad) died, I began thinking a lot about my adoption and my life.

I kind of always knew I was adopted. My family made it special and I didn't really see anything wrong with it. I was always excited to tell people. A lot of people gave me positive attention for it. They always answered my questions to the best of their ability and helped me understand. I was never angry or sad about it. I was just happy to be with them. They said, "Your birth parents couldn't take care of you, so they wanted you to have a better life and we found you."

My parents knew a family that had just adopted from Russia and had success, so they wanted to try. My mom was unable to have kids. I have two younger sisters also adopted from Russia (different parts of Russia and different biological families), and my mom was adopted from New Jersey, USA.

Since I talked about it from such a young age, I'm very open to talking about my adoption. People still think it's interesting and always want to know more. Adoption is not an easy choice, but it's what's best for the child in most cases. For me, it wasn't a sad life event. A lot of people say, "I'm sorry," if I say I'm adopted, and I say, "Why?" My life is so good here, and I have an amazing family and friends. There's nothing to be sorry about.

I actually had luck in meeting my birth mom and birth brother (father isn't in the picture). Though she knows some English, it's still hard to ask certain questions. I've asked her about mental health, because I have anxiety, depression, and other mental and physical disorders. But in Russia, I guess they don't believe in mental

Parents want nothing more than for their kids to love them back.

illness or think it's silly? And I believe she told me, "Oh no, here we don't use therapists or medication. When I'm sad, I drink. It's better." Hearing her say this made me sad. Russia is a different world. And after that, I didn't want to worry her with my problems. I would like to know more about my birth father. She hasn't opened up about him much.

My interests are not really affected by my adoption. Most of my hobbies are because I enjoy them. I did find out that my birth mom is an artist and brother is into culinary arts and producing music, so that's where I get my artistic abilities.

I believe your mom is the woman that raised you and took care of you. Same for father. I call my birth mom by her name, Lusha. I think people use the word *real* because that's your blood family. I get asked the same thing as other Russian adoptees do. Also, they ask if I speak Russian. Yeah, maybe I knew Russian fluently at ten months old, but I didn't keep it growing up in an English-speaking household.

I hear adoption jokes a lot. They don't really bother me unless it's directed at me and someone doesn't know. But no one has ever said anything bad about adoption to me. I've heard some bad stories from other adoptees. My best friend is adopted and her mom unfortunately died of cancer and had to give her up. Others had parents with drug issues and grew up with them till about seven years old. I've heard people make fun of them for that and bully them. I'm fortunate to not have had that happen to me. But one of the best things I've been told would be that people have said they are so happy I was adopted because if I hadn't been, I wouldn't be in their life.

I would tell other adoptees to embrace it. You were taken in by people that wanted a child. I understand some kids being resistant and confused. Some lash out at their parents. I know some people that rebel and actually hate their parents for adopting them. But their parents want nothing more than for their kids to love them back. So I hope they realize it's a blessing to be where they are now - not in foster care, orphanage, or in the streets. Now, your life is so much better.

HAILEY

My name is Hailey, and I'm adopted from China. I was nine months old when I was adopted, and I was in foster care. I am a twenty-one year old senior at Baylor University. I am pursuing a degree in Social Work. I am engaged to my fiancé and plan to work in Waco after graduation.

I feel as though adoptees and their families have this rich, unimaginably unique story that helps to shape their identity. As cliché as it sounds, adoption really makes the individuals involved in its process (adoptee or family member) special. And personally, as an adoptee, I think that adoption gives me a beautiful testimony to the power of love. I'm not sure if people who aren't familiar with adoption recognize that there's still familial love among adoptive families; there's this weird perception that parents won't ever *fully* love their children if the kids aren't their own flesh and blood. It's weird/complicated.

Anyhow, being adopted means that I have proof that true, familial love can be formed in non-traditional families, and I get to say, "Look - see how loved and cherished and blessed I am to be in an adoption-formed family!"

In my own journey, I have found that there is little that is hard for me to *accept* about my adoption. I think the most difficult thing for me is wondering where I come from. Who were my parents and why was I given up for adoption? It's not a heart-wrenching, chronic distraction, but the curiosity and nostalgia comes up every once in a while. When it does, I can reel my emotions back in pretty quickly.

When I look at the life I've been given here in the United States, anything that "may have been" seems obsolete. I have parents who have sacrificed so much to give me everything I need for success. I have a sister I love dearly (who was also adopted from China), and a man who loves me. If I hadn't been adopted, this life wouldn't be mine. I wouldn't trade it for anything.

In 1995, the "one child per family" law was still in place in China, so that could very well have been the reason I was put into adoption (assuming my parents already had a child). My age made my

I'm not sure if people recognize that there's still familial love among adoptive families.

adoption relatively easy. While my parents recall the stories of my resistance to being put into their care, apparently that didn't last very long. The first couple of days, I wouldn't even look at them.

By the time they returned to the USA, I had grown accustomed to being in their care. I was nine months old, so my memories of China are nonexistent. English became my first language, and I grew up with the impression that I was just as "white" as the next person (even though I knew I was from China). I grew up in a majority-White population and never really felt alienated.

I was adopted in a cohort of seven girls (myself included) with my adoption agency. We were the first children for all seven sets of new adoptive parents. In the two weeks that our parents were in China to adopt us, they became pretty close and decided that they wanted their families to continue keeping up with one another.

Every summer, all seven families choose a destination and meet there for a couple of days, so (in a way) I grew up with these girls. We don't do these annual reunions anymore but we did so diligently for the first thirteen years or so. I know this isn't really connected to my birth family or Chinese heritage, but it is a recollection of being reconnected with my "China cousins," the fictive-kin name our group *adopted* - pun intended.

I LOVE talking to people about adoption. I think it's really important to be willing to share your adoption story when possible. While I enjoy movies like *Despicable Me* or *Harry Potter*, their portrayal of adoption is *grossly* inaccurate. Because this is what society bases their perceptions of adoption off of, I think it's important to "set the record straight" as one who has gotten a true experience of the process.

Whenever I tell someone I am adopted, I also make sure they know that I am more than happy to retell my story. I think a willingness to talk about it also makes the process of adoption less foreign and scary.

Adoption is not about being "saved." I hear a lot of praise for adoptive parents as being "saints," giving the orphan a home and a family. While I totally agree that adoptive parents are wonderful beings deserving of all recognition, I also want people to acknowledge that adoption isn't just about taking a child in.

Personally, I don't think a lot of adoptions are rooted in a desire or calling to get one less child out of the system; adoption is about wanting to grow your own family. The relationship is reciprocal: the child blesses the family as much as they impact the life of the child. Wanting to adopt is a very intentional decision, and people never (or shouldn't) adopt to become a heroic figure; they do it to become a mother or father.

I don't care for the term *real* and, I mean, "Are my parents/sister real?" As opposed to what? Fake? I prefer using the terms *family* and *biological family*. I choose not to describe my family as "adoptive family" because it's sort of an isolating term. Non-adoptive families don't say, "Oh, that's my biological family over there!" I don't feel a need to say anything more than, "That's my family." My parents have housed, clothed, educated, disciplined, spoiled me. My sister has fought me, comforted me, kept my secrets, shared my clothes. We're just like any biological family. So, they're my family. Period.

I get asked if I know Chinese (especially at Asian restaurants or nail salons - HAHA). People ask me where I'm from and actually get mixed up with my ethnicity pretty often. They think I'm Filipino instead of Chinese. The question that's most annoying is, "Do you want to go back to China?" Maybe as a visit, but not to live there (which is what the asker is implying). Why would I leave my life behind? As for other things I wish I knew, I would honestly only want to know about my family's medical history in case there were any health concerns I should be aware of.

Haha, I love that you asked about adoption jokes! I'm not offended by them, although I'm sure this is one of the things that continues to misconstrue society's perception about adoption. My mom gets really upset by things like this and, in some instances, the notion of adoption is thrown out there in a crass/too-far sort of manner. But I'm not going to go off on someone who makes adoption jokes. Unless it's really offensive. Then I'll speak up.

The best thing someone has said about adoption to me was about the family dynamic. One of my friends said that some of the adoptive families he knew were the "tightest-knit families that God has ever made." And I definitely think that's characteristic of a lot of adoptive families. The baby's parents have to be so diligent and resolute in their pursuance of family-hood/parenthood. There's a promise to be nurturing and loving parents/family members.

My spiritual life has been impacted by my experience as an adoptee. I find the metaphor of being adopted into the family of Christ to be so overwhelming and hopeful. I know how loved I am by my earthly parents, I can't even imagine the love the Father has for us. I feel my adoptive family's love so strongly and evidently in my daily life. I know that it is no less than if I were a biological descendent. Ergo, I can see my church and (on a larger scale) Christians moving and working together as a family, never doubting that it may well be a similar, familial love as we're "adopted" into the family of God.

I'd just encourage people to do two things: ask questions and be sensitive. Yes, please. If you're curious, find an adoptee and ask them questions, as many as you can. We want you to be informed and unafraid. Adoption is a beautiful thing. On the same token, there are some adoptees who struggle with their stories and identities. If they are struggling to recall their stories or "don't know" the answers to your questions, leave it at that. Ultimately, it's their business, not yours. Adoption is still kind of a taboo, but until the subject becomes familiar (through education and open conversation), it will remain a means of "alienation" for adoptees and their families. Therefore, I strongly encourage curious individuals to ask their questions. I do love to tell.

HEATHER

My name is Heather, and I'm adopted. I'm twenty-one years old and currently a student at Wright State University. I study Sociology and Sexuality Studies. I'm in a sorority where I serve as Sisterhood Chair and Social Chair. Additionally, I'm an event planner with a focus in weddings. Above all, I'm a cat mom.

I was born in Ohio, adopted in Ohio, and raised in Ohio - I'm still in Ohio. I was adopted at five days old and I was in foster care for that five days while my adoption was being finalized. My adoption was opened (by me) when I was fourteen, so I communicate with my birth parents. I have a ton of family members, and I feel so loved. That's the best part.

The hardest thing for me, I think, was when I was taken from my adoptive parents and given to my grandparents when I was six. It was like being adopted twice, and it was really difficult. It still is, actually. I've gone to therapy off and on for years because of this.

My mom always ensured I knew I was the favorite by telling me I was picked by her. I wish she knew how hard it is to feel like you know nothing about yourself. I think that being a newborn in the system put me at a great advantage. Most people want an infant when they adopt; as you get older, your chances of adoption decrease.

I talk about my adoption a lot and always answer questions. It's something that's a big part of me, so I don't hide it. I wish people understood that just because someone is adopted, it doesn't mean they aren't their parent's *actual* child. I wholeheartedly agree that I hate the term *real parent* and wish people didn't use it. That's the actual worst.

It's difficult to grow up in a family where no one knows your medical history and where you don't look like anyone. I wish I knew how life would've been if my birth mother had kept me.

I left the Christian church at thirteen and ended up converting to Judaism. I think part of this was me finding myself.

I wish she knew how hard it is to feel like you know nothing about yourself.

I love being asked questions because I love the curiosity. I always get asked if I know my biological parents or talk to them and how old I was when I was adopted. I hate when people ask who my "real parents" are, that's so insulting to my family. I love almost every other question.

I hate jokes about adoption. They make me so uncomfortable. There's nothing wrong with being adopted, so why make it into a joke? The worst thing someone has said to me is that they wouldn't ever adopt because they want their kids to be "theirs." The best is when people tell me I'm special because I was the one they picked. It's actually pretty cool. That's about it, I guess.

JAKE

Author's Note: Jake did not fill out an interview but provided us with a testimony he had written in the past with updates. I'm deeply appreciative of his bravery in sharing his story.

Hi, I'm Jake, and I'm adopted. I was born in April, 1989 in Muskogee, Oklahoma. I wasn't born into an ideal home. My mom was a prostitute and a drug addict. To this day, I still have no idea who my dad is, but I have a feeling he was one of my mom's clients or boyfriends.

When I was born, my mom had no money and nowhere for us to live so we would stay at her clients' houses. That's when I started to be abused by her and her clients. I vividly remember being shoved into a corner and being continually hit with a fly swatter, being kicked, punched, slapped and thrown into objects.

In my eyes, this was love. Because I had never known any differently, I thought that this is what people do when they love you. But I was strong, I could endure it. But then my mom had a baby girl, my sister. I knew I could endure it, but now I had to protect her, too. So now I was being abused even more, I was now taking the punishment if my sister did anything wrong.

At this point in time, my mom, my sister and I were still bouncing around from place to place. When I was five years old, my mom met a guy named Freddie. For some reason, Freddie just had it out for my mom and me. If my mom did something that he thought was wrong, he would hit her, push her and throw her. After she was black and blue, he would come after me. I also remember Freddie trying to bust the door down and my mom holding my sister and me crying hysterically telling us that, "It's gonna be alright."

As my mom continued to get in trouble with the law, my sister and I were put into child protective services. We were taken four different times. My mom would go to court for her trials, she would cry and tell the judge, "I can change, I can change." The judge continually gave her more chances, but after the fourth time, she lost full custody of us.

I was terrified. I wondered why these strange people were taking us away from our mom. I remember being in the courtroom and sitting in the back pew and the judge saying something to my mom and her crying. She started walking down the aisle and then she grabbed me and gave me a big hug. Then they took me away. Little did I know that was the last time I was going to see her.

My sister and I lived in a foster home for a year. The foster parents were different. They showed love in a different way, which was something I wasn't too familiar with. They taught me how to ride a bike. I have a lot of good memories when I lived with my foster parents.

I remember playing video games with my foster brother and also being taught how to ride a four wheeler and a dirt bike. My foster parents were always the first ones up in the morning and they always had breakfast ready for everyone. When I started school, I was far behind, but they helped me as much as they could. I loved them.

The foster parents were different. They showed love in a different way, which was something I wasn't too familiar with.

After a year in the foster home, my sister and I were adopted. I was six years old. My adoptive parents wanted a little boy and they picked me, but my sister and I were a package and we came together. Because of that, they decided to adopt both of us. Once again, I was being taken away and I didn't want to be, but I didn't have a choice.

At first, I thought these people were nice. In some ways they were like my foster parents, but in more ways they were like my biological mom and all of her previous boyfriends. By this point, I had been exposed to a world that many adults have never even been exposed to and my mind was disturbed. It was very hard for me to trust men, well, really anybody. Because of this, I kept to myself and didn't allow anyone to connect with me. I felt alone, like no one cared for me.

When I turned seven, we celebrated my birthday for the first time ever. I had no idea what was going on. I thought to myself, "All of these people are here for me? This is all for me?" I felt like people cared for me and that people were starting to love me again.

A couple months later, my mom went out of state for business for nine days. Because people were always leaving my life, I thought she was leaving me, too. I was scared and thought, "It's happening all over again." I guess I did something wrong again, or didn't do something good enough, but all that I knew for sure was that my new dad started hitting me and hitting me. I guess he wasn't fully satisfied with just hitting me so he took me out back and locked me in the shed.

I thought I was getting a better life by coming here. I was wrong, but I was used to this stuff by now. I continued to think that this is what people do when they love you. I spent a lot of time in that shed on numerous occasions.

I started getting into trouble at school. It was almost like it gave my dad a reason to abuse me and he would look forward to it. Many times, he drove me out to the dock at a lake. He parked the car and told me, "Get the f*ck out of my car and start walking! You see that bench over there? Well, that's where you will be sleeping from now on."

As I cried hysterically, I got out of the car, walked over to the bench he had pointed at and laid down. This wasn't the only time he did this. He would drive off, and I would find myself all alone. He always came back, but sometimes not for hours. When he would come back, he would roll down the window and yell angrily for me to get back in the car.

As I climbed back into his truck, I would try to quit crying. He would reach over the arm rest, punch me in the stomach and say, "Quit crying," and would always make comments like, "Why did I ever adopt you?"

I was behind in almost every area of my life. In fact, I wasn't fully potty trained until the age of eight or nine. If I wet the bed or wet my pants, my dad would hit me so hard over and over again while saying, "That's disgusting! You should know better than that!"

Over the next couple of years, my mom's drinking got progressively worse. When she got home from work, her number one priority was drinking. She started to care about drinking more than us. My parents started fighting a lot, usually in front of us. It became a daily thing. I would try to break it up, but when I did, my dad would lash out at me.

One of the only good things about my mom being drunk was that she became remorseful about things and was caring. My dad went to many fishing tournaments. He would be gone weekends and sometimes even be gone for weeks at a time.

While he was gone, my sister and I would have to babysit my mom and make sure she didn't hurt herself. My mom liked to take baths while she was intoxicated, and my sister and I felt obligated to stay up with her, we were afraid she might drown or something. Sometimes my sister and I would stay up almost all night watching over her.

Whenever he would leave, she would take advantage of it and get more drunk than usual, so we would stay up all night taking care of her, but even this was better than being hit. I always looked forward to my dad leaving.

My dad's best friend from high school, Steve, was going through a divorce, so my parents let him stay with us for a couple of months. I was so excited, I loved him! He was funny and he would play games with us. While he was staying with us, my dad went on a fishing trip for a week. By this time, my mom and Steve were drinking buddies.

One morning, my sister came to my bedroom and woke me up. She told me that Steve was in bed with my mom and they were both naked. I went to my parents' room to see for myself, and sure enough, she was right. Their clothes were scattered all over the floor and, being twelve years old, I was smart enough to know that my mom had just had an affair. When my dad got home, I told him what had happened. My mom ended up confessing to it and the next thing I know, Steve was gone.

My parents made me go to church when I was growing up. I did confirmation when I was in the eighth grade, it didn't really mean that much to me, though. I had to take a test, and I didn't feel like I should have to do this. I felt like I had to take a test for God to love me, and if I failed, he wouldn't love me, and my whole life, I felt like I failed at everything I ever did, so I felt like he would never love me.

I could never really grasp the whole church thing, probably because everybody at the church that I went to was so judgmental that it just didn't seem real to me. Another reason I may not have grasped it was because it was so hard to believe in God after all that I went through. I thought if there really is a God out there, then why would he not have rescued me?

That same year, on Christmas Eve, my mom sat us down and told us that my parents were thinking about getting divorced. That is one reason why Christmas is a hard holiday for me. Not really because they might have been getting a divorce, but because I knew if they did, I would have to live with my dad, and I was afraid that he might blame me for his failed marriage and hurt me even more, or maybe even kill me. But, honestly, I was more worried for my sister than my own life, and I knew I wouldn't be able to watch over her.

Soon after, my mom went to rehab for alcohol abuse. I felt alone because people were always leaving my life. The eight weeks that she was gone my dad was very abusive towards me. When she got back, I was so happy to see her, but then I noticed that she had changed.

If there really is a God out there, then why would he not have rescued me?

Now she was sober, she was no longer remorseful or caring. Now, instead of screaming, "Stop! Stop!" when my dad was hitting me, she just simply left the room and acted like she didn't see anything. She no longer stood up for me and I felt hopeless. I can't tell you how many times I have wanted to kill my parents and how many times I have planned it over and over again in my head.

I also have had multiple thoughts of suicide and have attempted it several different times and different ways. My sister and I have also planned on running away, but were too afraid to. By this time, I was so hurt by these people, I just couldn't take it anymore.

My freshman year in high school, I played soccer and loved it so much. One of my teammates was a foreign exchange student from Germany. I invited him over to hang out and play video games. At least, that's what my parents thought. My parents had a liquor cabinet full of alcohol that they never got rid of. My friend and I wanted to drink, so I grabbed four of five bottles so we could get drunk together. We drank so much that I was throwing up all over the floor and laying in my own puke pile.

We fell asleep there and woke up to find my parents hovering over me. They immediately rushed me to the emergency room. I consumed so much alcohol that I had alcohol poisoning and they had to pump my stomach. Still to this day, I have no idea how much I drank or even if I might have been trying to kill myself. That night, I realized that there were things out there in the world that I could use to my advantage to suppress my pain and cope with everything I was going through.

You see, I was smart, so I thought ahead and hid a few bottles in my room just so I could get drunk whenever I wanted to. I loved the feeling of numbing my pain. I started to put alcohol in soda bottles and take them to school. I just couldn't cope with life anymore. I was doing poorly in school because my home life was so messed up. This was my escape time to do whatever I wanted without my dad being there with me. I thought that these new coping mechanisms were gifts from God, but, man, was I wrong.

That same year, I can remember a specific scene when my dad and I got into an argument. I left the room we were in, went to my room and slammed the door. The next thing I know, I hear loud footsteps ascending up the staircase as my dad is running to my room. He opened the door, ran toward me, and punched me in the stomach. He threw me on the ground and started laughing and making fun of me.

As he walked off, something in my head clicked. I was sixteen years old and had taken this from him way too long. I was no longer going to allow this to happen, so I decided to fight back. I punched him as hard as I could, first in the back, then when he turned around, I decked him in the face. Apparently my mom walked by the room right when I decked him the face. She automatically assumed that he didn't do anything wrong and that I started it.

The next thing I know, I'm being sent to anger management. I cried out to the counselor, in fact, I had cried out to a lot of people by this time. No one ever listened. No one ever believed me. No one ever stepped in. Even to this day, I wonder what they told our family and friends when I tried to cry out to them. I wonder if they told everyone I was lying or that I'm crazy. An excuse my mom used a lot was, "It must have happened in your past."

I had cried out to a lot of people by this time.
No one ever listened.
No one ever believed me.
No one ever stepped in.

I was so alone. In fact, I could never remember a time in my entire life when I didn't feel alone. Now that I had fought back, the physical abuse stopped; however, the emotional and mental and verbal abuse continued.

During my junior year, I started smoking weed. Everything spiraled out of control. I started skipping school. I would go to my truck and smoke a few bowls of weed, and sometimes I would go to friends' houses and get messed up. I started popping prescription drugs like they were candy.

I started to black out very frequently, sometimes they lasted for days. I would be at school and then I would open my eyes and I am at home or even back at school the next day. I started to learn that I could make myself black out even without the drugs or alcohol. It became my coping mechanism when I didn't have access to anything to numb my pain. It created an outlet where I was able to escape from my current situation. I no longer had to be present through the torment and misery. I had a way out.

Everything had gotten out of control. The first time I took Xanax, I snorted seven bars and combined it with alcohol, which is a deadly combination. I had relationships with new women, new friends, and certainly new enemies. This period of time was such a blur for me. I can barely remember anything that happened during this time but only things that people have told me.

I didn't care, I loved it. I had attention, I had sex, I had money, and most importantly, I had drugs. Everything revolved around getting my next fix. During this time, my new friends introduced me to acid, Ecstasy and coke. By this time, I was robbing people, stealing cars, setting them on fire, running them into people's houses and blowing things up. I was doing the most destructive things that I could possibly do to try and hurt as many people as I possibly could. I was so hurt inside, and I wanted others to hurt as well. Like the saying says, "Hurt people hurt people." The things I had done were all over the Oklahoma City news. I was a burden to society.

When I was eighteen, my parents found out about most everything I was doing and set me down in the living room. They gave me two options: seek help or move out. I think my mind was altered that night or maybe I was just fed up with these people.

But I moved out that night, I was finally free from them. A friend said I could stay at his apartment with him for a little while, so I moved in with him. By this time, I had such a high tolerance for the drugs that I had to do triple the amount of drugs I had started out doing just to get high. I did drugs anywhere I wanted to, and I wasn't scared of the cops or anybody else. I hurt so many people, and was so bad into drugs that I lost fifty-eight pounds and was down to one hundred and two pounds.

I would go days without eating and go days (even weeks) without showering. The apartment I was living in was so disgusting, there were cockroaches everywhere, moldy food that had been there for weeks, drugs, porn magazines, empty beer bottles, empty liquor bottles everywhere. Not to mention all of the throw up stains on the carpet. Not your ideal place to live. I was killing myself, but I didn't care any more. I was so tired of caring.

One day, my roommate and I got into a big argument where we were literally so close to killing each other. He kicked me out. I was homeless for a little while. I was sleeping on the streets, and if I was lucky, I would sleep in one of my friend's cars. Later, a guy that I worked with let me stay at his parents' house. He helped me when no one else would, and he saved my life.

I guess something just clicked, and I realized that I am better than this life or something, but I decided to use his phone to call my parents. I told them that I needed help. Surprisingly, they were willing to help.

They found an empty bed at a rehabilitation center. I stayed for about two months and got sober. I gained about sixty pounds, and I have never eaten so good in my life. After I completed my two months at rehab, I went to a halfway house. I hated it there. I felt like I was in a house full of junkies and it pretty much was just that. But, at least I had people I could relate to. We were required to attend Alcoholics Anonymous meetings twice a day.

I didn't really learn that much at the halfway house. It was hard to really get anything good out of that place, but I did learn one thing that stuck with me after I moved out: I didn't have a drug problem or alcohol problem, I simply had a screwed-up life, and I was doing all of the drugs and stuff to cope with everything.

I got unfairly kicked out of the halfway house for fighting, but it was a fight I didn't even fight in. By this time I was totally used to being wrongly accused and having to take the consequences. Once again, I was homeless and I found myself bouncing around friends' houses. After there weren't any houses left to bounce around to, I moved back to Oklahoma City.

I relapsed shortly after moving back to the city. I was sober for almost a year while in treatment and now I had just flushed it all down the drain. I started drinking and smoking weed again. One time, I smoked weed that was laced with something and it put me to sleep for two full days. When I woke up, I was at my friend's apartment laying in a pile of my own urine and poop. He kicked me out shortly after that, and this time, I really had nowhere to go. I was truly homeless. I had used up all my friends and I had no one. I slept on benches in parks, under bridges, anywhere I could find some sort of shelter.

I got a ride to downtown Oklahoma City, which is not a great part of town. I got dropped off at an insane asylum, not to be admitted, but because they would let homeless people stay on the first floor if the temperature was thirty-three degrees or less and snowing. I thought I was going to be able to stay there for the night, but the temperature was thirty-four degrees, so they would not let us in. I thought I was going to freeze to death that night or get robbed. I was so cold and had nothing to keep me warm. It just so happens that night was Christmas Eve.

I contacted my parents and they agreed to come pick me up and let me spend Christmas day with my family. I thought it was going to be great. I couldn't wait to see my grandparents, my aunts and uncles, my cousins, and most of all, my sister...but it was far from perfect. I sat there and watched as my sister got a brand-new, top-of-the-line cell phone, lots of clothes, pretty much everything she asked for and more. I received a ten dollar gift card to Walmart and it wasn't even from my parents.

I felt like no one even wanted me to be there and that nobody wanted the best for me. I was torn up inside. Since the day I can remember, my parents have always favored my sister over me. I'm always the one who got abused, I'm always the one who had to work for everything. Even still today, this is a problem for me. My parents have always idolized my sister over me. But they are either too blind to how bad this hurts me or just don't even care.

They wouldn't allow me to spend the night at their house, so my dad drove me back downtown and dropped me back off on the streets that night. He did ask me if there was any place that I knew of where I could stay. I thought about it and told him that there was a place called the Salvation Army that I knew I would have a bed at. He came and picked me up the next day and drove me an hour-and-a-half to Enid. By this time, I was used to being dropped off in negative ways.

I now had a place to sleep, food, and a couple of days later, I got a job at a local fast food restaurant. My goal was to save up money to get a car. This way I would be able to sleep in the car and then be able to save up for an apartment. Well, that didn't happen.

At the bottom of my suitcase I found an old number of a friend, Dave. He used to live in the halfway house with me, so I called him and he offered for me to come live with him. I agreed and moved in the same day. He wasn't sober anymore and neither was I. We started drinking, smoking weed, and doing Ecstasy together. His roommates were absolutely crazy, but I didn't care; I finally had a place to stay and as much alcohol and drugs as I could possibly want right at my fingertips. I was living the life.

Two weeks later, a girl named Haylee got kicked out of the halfway house and needed a place to stay. I had never talked to her before, but I knew who she was because I had seen her at meetings. We decided to let her come live with us. We had four people living in a ten by ten room, but I didn't mind. I still had drugs, alcohol, and now, a woman.

Haylee had been sober for eight months and as soon as she moved in with us, she relapsed immediately.

Next thing I know, Haylee and I started dating and doing drugs together. Five of us drove down to Dallas to go to a rave. I had a bad trip while we were down there and that was the final straw for me. I had said many times before that I would quit drugs, but this time I was serious. I told Haylee that I wasn't going to date someone that was doing drugs, so if she wanted to stay with me, she would have to quit, too. After a month and a half of using together, she quit with me.

A few months later, we moved out of that crazy house and got our own apartment together. Haylee and I were having unprotected sex, and five months after we started dating, we hit another speed bump in the road: she was pregnant. Everyone around us was telling us that we should give our baby up for adoption, but with my personal experience, that wasn't going to happen.

Haylee and I also did not believe in abortion, so we decided to keep him. My son Caleb was born on April 19th, 2010. I have never seen anything so beautiful in my life, and I loved him with all my heart from the minute I laid eyes on him. I realized when my son was born, that this is my chance to give him a life I never had, a life free from abuse and neglect. I realized it stops with me.

Both of our parents came to the hospital. I didn't want mine to be there, but Haylee didn't want any drama, so I agreed that they could come. When they held Caleb, I felt sick to my stomach and always made sure that I had an eye on them at all times. I didn't want to let them hold him, but I was trying to respect Haylee after all that she went through that day.

Over the next couple of months, I got really close to Haylee's family. I had never seen a family that was anything like them. They listened to me, they acknowledged me, and they accepted me for who I was. I was falling in love with her family. I looked at Haylee's parents and I could see how loving and nourishing they are, and then I looked at my parents in disgust, because I could see how destructive and cruel they could be.

After a couple of months, I realized how hard it was to be a father and I definitely wasn't ready for all of the responsibility. I started drinking again, not a lot at first, but it progressed very fast. I was lying to Haylee about where I was going, who I was with, and what I was doing. I started working eighty to ninety hours a week, and I wasn't getting much sleep when I was home because of the baby, so drinking was my outlet.

Within a week or so, I found myself drinking almost every day. I didn't have any good friends at the time that were positive or making anything of their lives, so I started living like them. All they did was drink, so I did, too. I started going to the bars and strip clubs pretty much every night with my friend from work. We would get wasted every time.

Haylee started to catch onto things and tried to call me out on it, but I just wouldn't admit to it. I didn't realize that I was hurting her and Caleb, and I was quickly distancing myself from them. I was becoming just like my parents, and I had always told myself that I don't want to be anything like them. That really scared me and was a big eye-opener for me.

Seven months after Caleb was born, I asked Haylee's dad for her hand in marriage. Even though she knew I was hurting her and our son, she said yes. She never gave up on me, and I couldn't believe I was going to be marrying her. I never thought I would ever find someone that accepts my screwed up life. I was always afraid if I found someone that I loved and could see myself with for the rest of my life, they would be too overwhelmed with my past history and leave me.

But Haylee accepted me for who I am, she wasn't turned off by my past. She helped me figure out who I am and helped me realize what I am capable of. I never pictured me getting married; frankly, I never pictured me living past or making it to the age of twenty-one. I was so thrilled that I had the permission to marry her. But even though I was really thrilled about marrying Haylee, I realized that all of my family would be at the wedding.

I thought to myself, "Hey, I could make a statement or speech about all of the events that happened in the past, I could expose my parents to everyone." Well, I ran that idea by Haylee and she quickly shot it down. After I thought about it for a while, I realized how horrible of an idea that was, so I didn't do it.

Haylee is from Dallas and we had grown really close to her family, so we decided to move down there. I still hadn't told Haylee all of the things I had done, and I didn't plan on it. Even though it was destroying me internally, I was used to hurting, so I endured it. We decided that if we were going to clean up our lives, this would be the perfect time. We quit smoking cigarettes, worked on our cussing, started going to church, and I worked on my drinking. I had been around smoke my entire life, so I never knew what it was like to not be around it, and trust me, I don't miss it.

Haylee grew up going to a church called Bent Tree, and when we moved down to Dallas in June of 2011, we started attending. We even had our wedding ceremony there. When I laid my eyes on Haylee when she was walking down the aisle, it was like I was looking at an angel. I have never seen something so beautiful in my life. It finally felt like everything was going the way it should, I was finally getting on track.

Haylee and her parents started talking about "The Bema." Honestly, I thought they were talking about a fish, but come to find out, it was a dramatic video Bent Tree made inspired by 2 Corinthians 5:10. When I was watching "The Bema," it hit me like a smack in the face. I felt a presence around me. It was a warm, tingly feeling, and something I had never felt before. I had felt the presence of God for the first time ever and I bursted into tears. I cried like a baby.

I didn't feel alone anymore. The feeling of emptiness that I had carried around with me for my entire life was now gone. A sense of security was finally with me. I had always claimed I was a Christian, but after that, I had truly found Jesus - I was saved!

God was teaching me so much. I was like a sponge taking in so much information, once I had opened my heart. I was also excited to make friends, and I realized I needed to come clean and tell Haylee about some of the things I had done.

I can't believe how much everything has changed over the past few years and how much better it's going to be in the future.

I had no idea what was going to happen. I was scared she might leave me, but I was willing to tell her the truth even if it meant risking losing her. By the grace of God, she forgave me. My marriage is so much better now. We both feel like we can connect on a whole new level now. My relationship with my son is amazing. We are so close now and I feel like he looks at me in a way I could have only dreamt of.

My relationship with my parents isn't perfect, but it is definitely improving. I never thought I would be able to forgive my parents. I am still working on not dwelling on the past and forgiving them. But I know that if I pray, and with the help of God, I will be able to completely move on and put everything in the past. I know I want them in my life, but mainly for Caleb's sake.

We recently found my biological uncle on social media, and I reached out to him, and then asked him about our biological mother. We talked on the phone and he filled me in that my mom committed suicide around 2001.

I had always questioned if she loved us, but he said she actually loved us so much, she tried to clean up her life to get us back. She had gotten sober, started going to church, but then found out she would never be able to see us again. She became so depressed by that knowledge, she decided to end her life. The only picture she had of us was on a shirt she had made and she died wearing that shirt with the original picture sitting on her chest. While this is obviously really sad, this gave us a lot of closure about how she felt about my sister and I.

My last foster family had always felt like family to me, and I felt unconditionally loved by them. Since then, foster care has always been on my heart. I talked with Haylee about it and the positive impact it had on my life. I wanted to have the chance to have kids in our house and have them know that they are loved and cherished, no matter how long they are with us.

We are currently about halfway done with our foster care classes and paperwork, looking to foster kids aged from about Kindergarten to fourth or fifth grade. We hope to be done with everything around December, and we will be getting licensed to foster and adopt.

God has transformed my life completely. He has impacted me to try and help as many people as I can that might be able to benefit from the circumstances I have been through. I know I am destined for something great, and I can't wait to see what that is. I can't believe how much everything has changed over the past few years and how much better it's going to be in the future.

JASON

My name is Jason, and I am adopted. I am a twenty-nine year old in business development and sales for start-up companies. After being born in LA, I moved to Dallas, Texas at age eleven, where I went to Highland Park High School, and then on to the University of Mississippi.

The best thing about adoption for me was knowing that my parents chose to have me, and being at a stage in their life where they were able to offer me a great deal of opportunity. They made it clear that they chose me, and I should feel extra special for that. The hardest thing about being adopted is trying to decide whether I ever want to have contact with my birth parents. Is that a path I want to go down?

I was born in LA, adopted prior to birth, and luckily both my adoptive parents were working there at the time to be able to adopt me through an agency. Since I was fortunate enough to be adopted before I was born, my parents are my real parents to me. They are all I know - my earliest memory.

My brother who is two years younger than me is also adopted. We do not discuss it much, I think he handles it differently than I do. He is much more open about it than me. I am not usually open about it unless I'm in deep or one-on-one conversation. It is kind of a sensitive issue to me, and people have so many questions. They will just fire off all these questions when they find out I was adopted. I wish that everyone understood that not everyone that was adopted comes from a traumatizing situation (i.e. broken home, orphanage, foster home).

It's worrisome not to have a full record of ones's health history. Are you predisposed to cancer, or heart attacks? I wish I knew what my birth parents do now. Are they still together? But I've had such a good life, ignorance is bliss for the most part.

My political views have been affected by being adopted. I'm certainly more pro-life because I am an adoptee. I would like to think I'm a productive member of society, and I could have been aborted just because my parents didn't want me.

[People] will just fire off all these questions when they find out I was adopted.

I don't like the term *real parents* either when people refer to my birth parents. My adoptive parents are my real parents because they are all I have ever known. They have given me everything in life. I prefer the term birth parents.

People always have a lot of questions, and they don't always realize it can be a sensitive and personal matter. Typical questions are: Where are your parents from? Did you live in orphanage? None of these really apply to my situation, nor do I have much information about my birth parents. Adoption jokes don't bother me unless they are directly aimed at me. I have pretty thick skin when it comes to jokes.

Worst thing said to me: "Your adopted your parents didn't love you."

Best thing said to me: Just people tell me that "I'm lucky," or they are genuinely interested in my adoption.

I feel incredibly lucky to be in the position I am, and not all who are adopted come from bad situations. I came from an incredibly loving home from day one, and my birth parents were able to provide me all the tools in life to be successful in the world because I was adopted.

JIMMY

My name is Jimmy, and I'm adopted. The name I have now isn't the name I was born with. In June of 1996, I was born in the Ural Mountains in the city of Nizhny Tagil under the name of Ivan. I do not know how long after I was put up for adoption, but I was placed in a local orphanage. Little did I know that, at the same time, an Italian-American couple from some odd five thousand miles away in the United States (Connecticut, to be exact) was looking to adopt a baby from Russia.

The orphanage sent them a VHS tape of me, playing with toys and being fed by the orphanage staff as I sat as comfortably as I could in the old rusty cribs jammed into the room. But this young Italian-American couple knew that I was the one. Through all the paperwork and travel arrangements, they flew halfway across the world about eight months after my birth to meet with me and sign me into their care as my parents. I traveled home with them nearly twelve hours on the plane, sleeping most of the way. The plane arrived back into the United States with one extra person than when they left.

We were greeted by my aunt and cousin in tears of joy, the first extended family members I would meet, and driven to a house that I would forever call my home. The place was packed with family and friends. Balloons and banners hung in every room celebrating my arrival into this new family. I was passed around meeting each and every person there until the wee hours of the morning, and not a minute did I cry or fall asleep (hinting at the fact that, to this day, I am still a night owl, haha).

Being raised Italian-American, I was introduced to many Italian words for simple kitchen items, homemade sauce, and some of the best family gatherings and food one could have. Religion was very important in both sides of the family, and from my first few weeks here, I was already attending Mass regularly. Most of my family lived a few towns away, if not in the same town, so family visits were common. In addition, my parents were doing well in their careers and were living a comfortable middle-class lifestyle in a mid-sized suburban town. This would become the town where I would grow up, meet my best friends for life, get an education, learn to drive, graduate, and where many other milestones would occur.

I have been supported and loved beyond belief by the family. They have driven me to become my best and given me such opportunity. I was taught by them to dream big, be ambitious, respect and love others, be peaceful, follow the law, and, most importantly, never give up. I still remember my grandparents teaching me the saying, "If at first you don't succeed, try try again." Today, I am who I am because of my family.

I love music. I played the violin for ten years. I love to DJ in my free time too. I was a swimming athlete on my high school team as well as captain and state qualifier. I host a radio show on my college campus and am involved in Phi Sigma Pi Honors Fraternity which helps the surrounding community. Most importantly, I was given the opportunity to attend college in Boston, MA to study Architecture in a five-year Master's Degree program.

I feel blessed that my life has gone the way it has. I sometimes think about the probability of how my life went, where I grew up, who I met, etcetera, and can't help but be in awe of how small the chances are. No words can show the appreciation that I have for all that I have been able to do in my life by now. I think about how different it would be if I had not been adopted and had remained in the streets of Russia trying to survive for myself. The way my life has gone has been such an amazing miracle.

I was very lucky to be adopted by two outstanding and supportive parents from Connecticut. I have been given ample opportunities in my life that I would not have had the chance to have if I was not adopted and remained as an orphan in Russia. I find the hardest thing to deal with is the thought of where I get my traits from. As an Architecture student in college, I cannot help but think if either of my parents were artistic in any way. I also wonder about my physical traits. Which side of my family does my blonde hair come from? Which of my parents gave me my facial features, like my jaw line or my eye color? Although these questions are always in my mind, I find that, believe it or not, questioning more like those above help me deal with the fact that I don't know. It drives my curiosity and eagerness to hopefully one day meet them again.

In all honesty, I cannot remember the first time I was told that I was adopted. Due to my young age at adoption, I was always aware of it, as my parents showed me the photos and videos of the day I arrived as part of the family since I was very young. I have always come to accept it easily, and I would advise other parents adopting children at young ages to ingrain the truth in their children's mind as they can grow and learn more as they become older. It helps, in that the child is not thrown the truth all at once at an older age. They may feel like they have been lied to by ones they love for a very long time. I wish they were able to find out or know if I have any brothers or sisters, or if my parents, uncles, aunts, or grandparents are alive today. I have a whole other family out there related to me which I haven't met, and am eager to know the location of any of them.

I feel that due to being adopted at such a young age of a mere eight months old, it has made me feel less connected to the country of Russia. Hence why I don't remember much at all. But the photos and videos show it all. Yes, I feel connected by my culture and family who live there, but I had been there a very short time as a baby and have no memory of my time there. This has helped me feel comfortable with my adoptive family and home here in the United States much easier than a child adopted at an age where they can recall their time in Russia. I feel that I have always lived here in the USA. There are no memories that come back to pull me back to my birthplace.

The thought of being taken away from all you know, your home, your family, and brought to a new environment can be scary and overwhelming.

I am the only adoptive family member and I am absolutely open to talking about my adoption! Many people do not know what it is like to be adopted, and I do try and share and open their minds to as much as I do know about my own adoption. I take pride in my adoption. Not to mention, many jaws drop when they find out I came from halfway across the world, haha!

I wish others could understand that adoption isn't "amazing" as they think when I tell them. Yes, I was very lucky and was adopted by a very supportive and loving family, but not all children are, unfortunately. My story may seem like a fairy tale to some other adoptive children, and I feel very fortunate and appreciate of all that I have been given in my life. Adoption can be life-changing for many, especially if you remember it. The thought of being taken away from all you know, your home, your family, and brought to a new environment can be scary and overwhelming. As an adoptee, I recognize that could have been me and respect all adoptees.

Luckily, my health has been in excellent shape for the last twenty or so years here. I have had no major illnesses, diseases, or life-threatening injuries (KNOCK ON WOOD). While I have been blessed with such stellar health, I do have concerns as I begin my adulthood. I wish to find out my medical history, so that I can stay ahead of it and plan in order to help offset any issues I may be genetically prone to receiving.

Siblings is also another one of my major questions. I grew up as an only child. My parents did not have any children or adopt any other children. I have never had the feeling of having a brother or sister. Others may say I was "lucky" not to have to share with a sibling when I was a child, or for other reasons, but I disagree. I envy the feeling of closeness one has with their siblings as it is something that I have never been able to feel. Finding out if I had a sister or brother in the world all these years would be amazing. It would also be satisfying to put to rest the question, even if I was an only child. I question the location of my family members and if they are doing well. Imagine meeting your mother or father for the first time after twenty plus years. It is a feeling even I cannot begin to imagine. I hope that both my parents and any other family members, are safe and healthy today.

I was raised in a Catholic household and family. Both sides of my family are religious and regularly attend Mass, as did I as I grew up. I do not know what religion, if at all, I would have followed if I had not been adopted. While I am not an avid churchgoer at my age right now in life, I do believe in faith.

I totally agree I don't like the term *real* parents!!! But, I don't even call my adoptive parents "birth parents" because they are *my parents* to me. They are all I have known all my life. While I respect my birth parents and family, I do see my adoptive parents just like any child adopted at a later age would see their birth parents. My adoptive parents are the only parents I have known, so I cannot begin to think of them as below my blood relatives. I like the terminology "adoptive" parents and "birth" parents. By using the word "real" to describe birth parents, it discredits the family who adopted and raised you.

Adoption is not a joke. PERIOD. While I was lucky to be adopted into such a family, many adoptees were not. I see and respect that fact. I am part of a social media group of Russian Adoptees, and many adoptees post that they struggle with their adoptive parents and living situations. My story has a happy ending, but not all do.

I was at a restaurant for a friend's birthday. The restaurant's theme revolves around the idea of shaming its customers for their looks and background. They put giant white hats with writing on them and put them on their guests' heads. It is supposed to be a fun and funny environment, filled with jokes and snarky comments by the staff. The waiter made paper hats with hate-comments written on them, individually for each person.

It was my first time there, and I had heard about this being the theme of the restaurant and knew what to expect. However, someone at the table decided to share to the waiter that I was adopted from Russia. Immediately, the waiter began to bash on me about it, as it is part of his job. But he clearly did not know when to stop or that certain topics have boundaries. I was told things like, "Your parents didn't love you enough to keep you, you would have been a disgrace to the family name," or, "Go back to the slums of Russia where you belong." I even was told things like, "They should have aborted you when they had the chance."

I was appalled that anyone would go to such a length on a topic that can be so sensitive to people, even if he was required to make fun of his guests. It seemed too far. As you read before, I am open to talking and educating people on the subject of adoption. But this crossed the line.

On the other hand, the best things I have ever heard are just the fact that someone respects when you share your story with them. Even if it's just "Thank you for sharing with me," it means the world that someone listens and respects that the person they know is adopted. No other words can show up the feeling of respect felt from another on this topic.

Being adopted is something I don't think about much. It comes into my head at random times. But I carry it with me everywhere I go. Sometimes I look at a family photo of someone I know and think how wonderful it is to know your blood relatives. How wonderful it must be just to simply physically look like those around you. It seems silly, but it's such a curiosity for me. What is it like to see someone who shares many physical features with you? To look at someone and know that you carry on their genetics, and have so much in common with them. I envy such a feeling that I have never felt, and hopefully one day, I will be able to look across the room at my mother or father and understand.

KARA

My name is Kara, I am twenty-three, and I am living in Dallas, Texas. I own my own furniture company. I don't know anything different since I was adopted at birth - so to me, it is what it is!

My parents were open about the adoption from day one so I am just used to it. My brother is biologically related to me and is also adopted. People are curious about my adoption, so I am open to talking about it. But I don't want anything to do with my birth family. I call them my "sperm donors" versus "my family" to be funny - they were only responsible for my conception, that's all my birth family is to me. Though I would like to know about major health risks.

I probably wouldn't have been religious nor had a career if I wasn't adopted. All of my birth family dropped out of high school, had kids at a young age, and did drugs. I just know how they are versus to how I am.

Does it bother me if people ask about my birth family? Meh, doesn't bother me. People just ask if I know them, and I say yes. But, I don't care to stay in contact with them. I wish they would stop trying to talk to me all the time. My family now is who my family is, not them.

KATHRYN

My name is Kathryn, and I am currently finished with college, now working in DC. And I was adopted over twenty years ago from Russia. I was two (almost three) and in an orphanage. Currently, I reside in Maryland. I live with my family that includes two older sisters, two brother-laws, two wonderful parents, and my boyfriend. I have had quite the journey these past twenty-one years, and I am learning and growing.

The best part about being adopted has been having the life I couldn't process as a baby to understand my circumstances. I have been given a life that has been wonderful with two loving parents and two older sisters.

Being adopted comes with its challenges, including explaining to non-adoptees what being adopted is like. They don't fully understand it. I think of where I am now to be a blessing, and I don't know where I'd be without my parents. They are the reason I am still living and proof that adopted children can survive and become something.

I think when I was old enough to process it was when they told me, and today I am more curious. I don't think it would have been a good idea to tell me when I was much younger. They were smart in that way. I think that it's hard to know about the life I could have been living if I had stayed with my relative in Russia. I was too young to fully understand what was happening to me. It's hard to see.

I am proud of where I come from regardless of the circumstances. I think, in the beginning, when I was in high school, I was guarded when bringing up my past, because I didn't know where I came from really except for the region. Now that I am older, I am more open to sharing that my journey hasn't been easy, but it's something that I try to explain to potential parents wanting to adopt to let them know that adoption is a wonderful thing.

I wish people could understand that every day is never that easy. I think adoptees put up a good front and don't always know how to express to those that don't understand that being adopted comes with its territories of problems that eventually get better over time, but this is something that I would think would be helpful for people to know.

In the past year, I have discovered more about my mother and how my uncles helped take care of me during conditions that were difficult. Apparently, my grandmother is in a psych ward. (Still trying to verify this.)

My faith in God has been influenced by my adoption. I believe He brought me to this wonderful family that took me in as their own. I do know there is a purpose at some point in my life because of my family finding me.

"Real family?" This part is the most complex part, because, not that I don't consider my birth parents (wherever they are) to be my "real family," I just never grew up with them to know them like I know my forever family that I *live* with. So, when I say "family," I refer to the family who raised me because that's who I am and have been for the past twenty-one years. Even though there may be another family out there, to me they are distant right now.

In the doctor's office, they will ask about my family/medical records, and I always tell them I don't know because I honestly don't know. There's still so much I don't know.

I have had some incidences where a joke about adoption wasn't funny - it really hurt. It also depends on if it's said by someone within my family. I don't take them too seriously when they are joking with me, but outside of my family it's different.

I haven't really had a lot of negative remarks because most of the people that I tell are understanding and tell me that I am so brave to have turned out the way I am because of adoption. In the fourth grade, I had an incident that I still remember to this day. A girl in my class was mad at me for something...she then stated out loud so people could hear, "At least my mother didn't give me up..."

This hurt so much, I walked right out of the room. I remember that hurt so bad to the point where I made it known that she said those remarks. Even though I was bitter then, I moved on from that, and the next day, she wrote me a card and gave me a dollar to apologize. I had three of the best friends who supported me and were there for me especially during that time. So, even though that was a hard time for me, part of me felt grateful for my friends then who knew me.

Being adopted isn't a privilege…
We deal with more pain because of the past.

Being adopted isn't a privilege. Every story is unique and different. I know some people who are adopted may not want to share or know their history, but it's been interesting because I never thought I could actually be happy. People who aren't adopted don't know what that's really like, and that is really hard. I think that the older we get, we deal with more pain because of the past, but it's more about what we bring to our futures. I am forever grateful for my past because I wouldn't be where I am today.

Being adopted is like a sacrifice when you don't fully know your own life but sometimes it's good to not want to know everything. I haven't had an easy year to process learning new information about my potential family. I also celebrate my Adoption Day every January 31st, which is when I came home. It's something to remind me of how far I have come. The older I get, the more I see this journey that could have been different. It's exciting, but so many mixed emotions.

My parents have really influenced me to want to adopt a child as well. Whether it be from Russia or somewhere else, it's something that makes me proud to admit I want to do. I realize the numerous sacrifices my parents had to take to get me. I am truly so appreciative of every little thing they have done for me.

I came with complications. I had bad ears, growth deficiency, a scar on my forehead, and malnourishment issues. All these areas of problems were fixed mostly right away and over time when I came to America. Coming to America was the best thing to happen to me. I realize also that even though money is something people worry about, I love the fact that my parents never really admitted how much it cost to get me. They would always say "you didn't cost anything." It was more of the experience of finding me than it was about the money.

My mom found the first photo that they were sent of me; they had asked if they could have a new one since I actually looked not so good in the photo, and yet they still wanted me - that's true love. I am who I am today because of adoption, and there is no looking back, it's more about looking forward and finding my own journey. If I find out about my birth family, that would honestly be a dream come true. Part of me still has some reservations, because I don't want to get too attached to the birth family. But I know what I want in my heart.

I love my life and take nothing for granted because of being adopted. It helps me be more thankful for my life. I am more connected with my parents that I live with today because they are my family, and no one can take that away from me.

KENDRA

My name is Kendra. I was born in Khabarovsk, Russia in October of 1996. I was adopted from an orphanage at the age of five-and-a-half months in April of 1997, and I have lived in North Carolina most of my life, so I consider it my home.

I don't really think there is a best thing about being adopted. Some people might disagree but I guess that mostly has to do with life, upbringing, and personal experiences. But the hardest thing for me has to be knowing that there was someone out there in the world that gave birth to you, and then something happened that they couldn't keep you, and there is family out there that you know of but can't see. There are not just birth parents, but possible siblings, grandparents, aunts, uncles, cousins, etcetera. I still deal with this to this day, and sometimes I find myself feeling alone and abandoned. Dealing with this is an everyday struggle, but I have to try to stay positive.

For my birth parents: I would like them to know that I never worried about basic necessities. I never worried about whether I would eat three meals a day, I always went to the doctor when I was sick, I was not concerned with being clothed, warm, or neglected. I wish my birth parents would have given me more personal information about them.

For my adoptive parents: I wish they knew that their lack of support and open disapproval of my self-discovery is very hurtful. I wish they knew how much I want them to stop trying to hinder my quest for answers and insight into my past. I wish that they knew the times when they disregard my heritage or when my "off the cuff" comments about being Russian are reprimanded...how hurt, annoyed, angry and disrespected I feel.

Being from a different country and seeing things on the internet about Russian woman and how they look and act, I've found myself picking up on things from that. An example would be that I've always been strong, even when I was young, and I've heard that Russian woman tend to be physically strong. Things like that. I was adopted so young I think that I've thought about what my life could have been like if I was adopted when I was a little older. Then I could have seen the place where I was born myself instead of through pictures. No one else in my family is adopted.

It really depends on the person I am talking with whether I am open to mentioning my adoption. In general, I don't talk to strangers about it in detail because it is so personal. If someone finds out that I am adopted, I'll answer their questions, usually bluntly and matter-of-fact so they don't try to go into the deeper more personal questions, and people tend to get the hint. I don't appreciate when people lump all adoptions and adoptive life together as a whole.

What do I wish I knew that I don't know? Everything. All the way down to the things that seem insignificant to other people but aren't to me. How much did I weigh when I was

I shouldn't feel guilty for wanting to know where I come from.

born? What do my parents look like? Who do I resemble the most? What mannerisms do I have from my mom versus my dad?

Most people assume that once a couple or person has chosen to adopt, then they have a "hero morality," yet there are often people who adopt and then fail to continue raising their adopted child with the same selfless, nurturing passion, and love that is assumed to be part of the adoptive parent's character. Adopting a person is the first step, then raising the child through adolescence is just as important as being adopted or "saved" as an infant.

I dislike when people tell me that I shouldn't be sad or angry with unanswered questions or longing for that unseen void filled, and that I should "be thankful and grateful, because I was one of the lucky ones that was adopted." This makes me feel very guilty and invalidated. Now that I'm older, I wish people would understand that I shouldn't feel guilty for wanting to know where I come from and a desire to talk freely. Wanting these things should not be treated as an ungrateful or shameful thought.

I haven't made decisions in my daily life based on being adopted. Being adopted never held weight in what I enjoyed, my daily routine, or what I wished to accomplish as a whole. I feel that people who were adopted under twelve months old don't know anything else but the family that adopted them. I believe that your family is who you grew up with and who was around you. So the kids that were adopted at an older, more impressionable age, I can see them feeling differently than I do because they might still remember their birth family.

I seem to shut down questions pretty quick. Commons questions I get asked are:

1) Do you remember where you were?
2) Do you speak Russian?
3) Do you remember your parents?
4) Do you have any siblings?

With adoption jokes, it depends on the joke. I take them individually and whether or not they are meant offensive or just carefree and superficial. I have encountered both.

The worst words spoken to me regarding adoption all pretty much center from my adoptive mother. That is an entirely separate and lengthy conversation. As far as the best words? "Regardless of the reasons that led to you being put up for adoption, there is no doubt that your birth mother made that choice as a selfless person." Hearing this perspective was very helpful when I am frustrated.

LARA

Author's Note: Now it's my sister's turn to share her story! Unlike our other interviews, this is her real name.

My name is Lara, and I'm adopted. I am twenty-one years old. I just graduated from Texas Tech University, and I'm now in graduate school for mental health counseling. I think I was just in an orphan area of a hospital, and I was one year old.

The best thing is getting to tell people that I am adopted from Russia. People always find that to be interesting. I also love having a great life that I probably wouldn't have had if I had NOT been adopted. The hardest thing for me is not knowing anything about my birth family or why they put me up for adoption. I haven't really dealt with it. I just don't think about it.

Honestly, I don't know what has helped me the most because I feel like I've just always grown up knowing that I'm adopted. I think maybe the fact that they (my parents) just always have told us we were adopted has helped me understand it. I feel like we are open about that topic. I've just always known I was adopted, so I grew up with a very normal life. I just say what I wish they knew when I'm thinking about it, rather than holding it in.

I am always open to talking to people about adoption because I love being adopted. I think it's cool and special. I think people should be more educated on the experience, so I'm always willing to share. I wish everyone could know that not everyone ends up emotionally scarred or distant from their parents. You *can* live a very normal life. It's something to take pride in, not be ashamed of.

You can live a very normal life. It's something to take pride in, not be ashamed of.

I would love to know ALL of my immediate birth family: mom, dad, siblings. I think it would be cool to be able to tell them about my life and everything. I also would like to know my medical history, so I can know if I am at risk for things like cancer or high blood pressure and whatnot.

Has anything in my personal life been influenced by my adoption? No, nothing has been influenced like that. I mean, maybe my religion. My parents who adopted me are Baptist. So am I, but, otherwise, I don't think being adopted has directly influenced it.

With family terms, I say "real parents," but I usually use "air quotes" with it because then I usually say "birth parents" right after. I tend to say, "Oh, I'd love to meet my parents. But they are my birth parents, because my adopted parents are my real parents since they raised me."

I always get asked if I remember anything, but no, I don't, because I was an infant. I also always get asked if I have any siblings. Or I get asked if my sister, Elena, is my blood sister. I don't hate any questions or love any in specific. I mostly respond to any and all questions. I guess I hate being asked, "Do you wish you knew your birth parents?" because it makes me sad and it is hard to talk about.

What do I think about jokes about adoption? I LOVE THE JOKES! Half of the time, people don't know I'm adopted. When they say an adoption joke, I say, "Yeah, I am adopted," and they feel so bad! I end up laughing, and I say, "No, I don't care, hahaha!" If the joke is said to people who are not adopted, then I'm kind of offended because the joke is not even an accurate statement about being adopted. They do not know what it is like.

No one has honestly ever said anything negative or bad about adoption to me. I guess one of the best things someone has ever said to me is, "Wow, that's cool you're adopted!" It's kind of a self-esteem booster. I don't feel bad about being adopted, but it's just great to know that other people think your adoption is cool.

It's just great and awesome to tell people about my story. I love when people are so encouraging. I hope to one day go back to Russia to visit the country and maybe find my birth family.

LAUREN

My name is Lauren! I'm twenty-three years old, and I was adopted from a Moscow orphanage when I was ten months old. I have one brother. He is the biological son of my parents and he is four years older than me. We have two dogs, Sasha and Peanut. I graduated from Ohio University in Athens, Ohio. I currently work for American Eagle's corporate office.

According to my documents, my birth mom left me on a table three days after I was born. Then she left the hospital through the first story window. I find this so interesting.

Seriously, my documents say this. It makes you wonder why that was how she gave me up. My dad knew someone who worked closely with the adopt-a-child agency in Pittsburgh and my great-grandparents are Russian. The decision was easy for them to choose Russia.

I think the best thing, however, is having a home, love, support, and a family. I love having a story, because it makes me more interesting, haha. I think the best thing about being adopted is bringing that insight about adoption into people's lives who meet me - who may not know anyone else who has been adopted.

I hate the unknown...I deal with it by keeping it channeled as intrigue and wonder rather than focusing on sadness and confusion.

I was very young when I was adopted. I think the hardest part is all the unanswered questions I have. All the unknown parts of myself. I hate the unknown. I only know four things about my birth mom and that's it. I deal with it by keeping it channeled as intrigue and wonder rather than focusing on sadness and confusion. When you view things in a brighter light, it makes them less heavy and dark. You could read my birth mom leaving via the window as a dark and tragic thing or you can just smile and thank God she did.

I wish my parents knew just how thankful I am for them. I've known about my adoption since before I can remember. My parents did a phenomenal job at making it a normal part of my life. I had baby books that revolved around Russia and adoption. I asked to see my records.

My dad handed me the manila envelope filled with my documents and said to me, "I know you already know all of this. We do not know how much of it is fact. It will be harder to read on paper. Your mom and I will be in the other room if you don't want to read it alone, are sad, or have questions. We love you and we will hold your hand through it all."

That was the most impactful.

Since I was ten months old, I am lucky to not have had a memory of my time before with my family. I do know if the first ten months had a long-lasting impact on my personality. I never ran to my parents when I was scared or sad, instead I self-soothed. We think this was because I didn't have someone to constantly tend to my needs as an infant. There are other things about my personality that I believe were influenced by my past. While they are not in my immediate family, I also have two cousins who were adopted from America.

Also, I think my desire to help people and animals could be influenced by being adopted, but I don't have any hobbies or jobs that stem directly from it.

I'm absolutely open to talking about my adoption with people. I find it interesting, and I love people's reactions. I also think being open about my adoption has helped me deal with the more difficult aspects of it. I wish people knew that we (adoptees) are all grateful, but that doesn't mean adoption is a fairytale all the time. A lot of adopted kids miss out on the most important time to connect with parents and your environment. Emotional, mental, and physical issues are real and do indeed exist within most adopted children - whether they are apparent or not.

I would love to know more about my birth mom and siblings. I think that would be the most interesting thing. Just to hear their stories and see where they've been. I've always been so interested in that.

I agree 110% that I dislike the term *real family*. I have one family. My mom, my dad, my brother, my aunts and uncles, etcetera. My birth parents and siblings are just my birth family. I hate the word *real* because there is no *fake*. There is just fact. I have a family and I was born from another. I wish people would understand there is no *real* or *fake*, they are both very real.

People ask me if I know Russian or if I can speak Russian; the only reason I hate this question is because I'm sad the answer is still no. I will try to learn the language eventually. I love when people ask me what I know about my adoption. I have a pretty surreal story in that my parents had a very hard time with the adoption process, and also what my documents say about my birth mom and what they know.

I don't mind jokes about adoption, really. My brother would tell people I was adopted and they would look appalled that he would joke about it, but then he would say, "But, no, really! She really was adopted!" He didn't mean it as a joke.

The worst thing anyone ever told me would be that, "You should go back to Russia because nobody wants you here… oh, wait, nobody wants you there either." And once, my brother and I were in a fight, and he always accidentally refers to our parents as just "*my* parents," but I said "*our* parents," and he said (in anger), "No, Lauren, you were adopted, remember? You don't have parents." That was hard.

The best comments I get about adoption are more common and pretty standard about being lucky and fortunate and that my parents chose me.

I think more people need to be educated on the adoption system and process, along with understanding the ramifications adoption can have on the child. I think people get so fixated on the fairytale of it all that they look down upon the adopted kids who are having a harder time because they chalk it up to being ungrateful. This is not the case, and I cannot stress that enough. Even those of us who fight with our parents or have had more trouble fitting into our families, this does not really make us ungrateful.

MIKE

My name is Mike. I'm sixty-three years young with four adult children: Tyler, Martha, Jared, and Mark. Married five times, most recently to Christine for a year now. Jared and Mark are full siblings. With Christine's two children and their spouses, we have sixteen grandchildren. Oldest grandchild is Tyler's daughter Briana. After graduating high school in 1971, I enlisted in the Marines and did three years active duty. My first wife left my son and I, so I got honorably discharged, moved back to Kansas City to work for my dad and raise my son. I work in construction, have for over forty years now.

I was born in Kansas City, Missouri and was an orphan for three months at St. Anthony's Orphanage. I was adopted through Catholic Charities by James and Vera. My parents were two very prominent figures in the community. My father was the owner and president of a large Union construction company, and my mother was director at a large hospital. My dad's father emigrated from Italy in 1901 with his brother and started a sheet metal company that later settled in Kansas City.

My parents also adopted my sister June in 1955 and brother Don in 1963, also from Catholic Charities. We were not blood siblings but told from very early age that we were "chosen," and it was no secret in the large Italian family, and

Keep searching your roots! You'll never know what you might find.

although us three were the only adopted ones, it was never even discussed and we were all family.

My parents provided very well for the three of us. My dad built a very nice, large custom house in 1953, I went to private Catholic Elementary and High School, and had everything I needed but not everything I wanted. All my life, I did kind of wonder what the story was about my adoption. I asked my mom a few times growing up, but she said that she had no information about anything. So, in my mind, I figured my birth mother got pregnant at a very young age and sent off to have the baby then returned to wherever. I couldn't have been more wrong.

While working on a construction project in October of 2014, I was hurt on the job. There is a pending case at this time with Work Comp and Civil Courts. My injury was a torn rotator cuff and torn bicep tendon and required surgery. The pain was intense and never-ending. While waiting over a year for my employer to allow me medical treatment, I was fired, had zero income for over a year and had *quite* a stressful life. I had Mark attending a private college and, of course, all other bills to pay. Thus, I developed a heart condition because of the pain and stress. Not ever knowing about any family health history, I thought it was a real good time to find out.

I hired a Search Angel for $200 to open up my adoption records. She told me that if my birth parents were alive, that they would have to give permission to release any info. She called in a week, saying that both of my biological parents had passed. My birth father passed in 2003 and birth mother in 2009. She sent me the identifying information, with an interview of my mother at St. Anthony's Orphanage. It told details about my father, his likes and talents. They both worked in KC as city bus drivers, and that is probably how they met.

She also told me that my father had been a City Councilman and a developer. He was a builder who had built a few neighborhood developments in outlying communities, and she actually lived across the street from him in one of his developments. He was well-known locally, and owned some businesses in that city.

The Search Angel then told me that I did have some siblings, and asked if I would like to contact them. I said, "Sure, why not?" So she told me to write a letter that she would send along with another letter from her, telling them about herself and give them her contact information. In my letter, I wrote that I was basically trying to obtain any medical information and meant no disrespect or harm. I included my phone number, email and address as well as social media stuff. Because I knew they would be checking me out very soon. The letters were sent to the Search Angel, and boy, did my phone start "blowing up."

This discovery has only been revealed in the past year, and gets more interesting every day with more discoveries uncovered. On my father's side, the younger siblings did not know of the older ones and vice-versa until I exposed the *real* story on both sides. But all have been wonderful and gracious to me, and it has answered many questions that they had.

I had a family reunion at my house for everyone on my mother's side last summer. Brothers and sisters got to meet for the first time. And the siblings on my father's side held a reunion for me, where everyone got to meet "the new brother." I also started a private social media group so we could share pictures and stories with each other. I can't tell you how much joy and love the families have enjoyed with learning and becoming parts of each others' lives now. We all talk on social media almost daily now. I know that many of these reunions don't go as wonderful as ours, and I know I am blessed.

It has really been quite a ride this last year learning more and more. On my bio-father's side, he had three children from 1940 - 1944 that they put up for adoption in 1944, then married. I still am trying to locate those siblings. After DNA testing, I found out that, although I was raised by Italians, I have zero percent. Norwegian! I also discovered that my fourth great-grandparents on my father's side were on the *Mayflower* with four other families of descendants. So, if you're adopted like me, keep searching your roots! You'll never know what you might find.

MIRIAM

My name is Miriam, and I'm adopted. I was born and three days later, I left the hospital with my adopted family. I am now a twenty-three-year-old who graduated from Baylor University in May of 2016 with a degree in Education. I am now an English teacher and I absolutely love what I do!

When I was in high school, I went through a very rebellious stage, which I think stemmed from my adoption. I was told that I was adopted when I was going into kindergarten, but I don't think I really thought about it much until my sophomore year of high school. That was the year where I guess I was really becoming who I was as an individual, and I was absolutely nothing like my adopted sisters were.

I think that every time my mom critiqued me or tried to advise me, I took all her comments as, "You're not like your sisters, why can't you be more like them?" which was very unfair to her. That is not what she was saying. I just wanted to be my own person and not have to fit into a pre-determined mold. I got out of that idea by embracing who I was and finding joy in the differences in my family instead of panicking that I was always disappointing someone by being different.

One semester of college, I failed a class, which none of my sisters had *ever* done. This was out of my rebellious and irrational high school stage, so I finally had a talk with my parents that I struggled with school and things didn't come so easy for me as it did for my sisters. My parents finally had the ability to tell me that they didn't care that I was different than all of my sisters and proceeded to point out that all four of us were so different from one another, I had just been looking at myself against all three of them instead of all of us as individuals.

My parents never really seemed to like talking about my adoption, or it just never came up with them after they told me when I was young. So, I guess I wish they knew how much I appreciate that they took me out of what could have been such a terrible situation and gave me everything I ever needed.

My biological mother was fourteen when she got pregnant with her nineteen-year-old boyfriend. They were going to keep me and raise me together, but then my birth dad ran away and they never heard from him again.

At that point, I guess my birth mom thought she couldn't handle raising a baby on her own, so she was going to get an abortion. My adopted family wanted to adopt, but that family already included two parents and three sisters. Adoption agencies wouldn't let them adopt a baby because they weren't really "in need."

My dad was a lawyer, and my biological grandmother happened to be one of his clients. When my biological grandmother learned about her daughter wanting an abortion, and my dad's struggle in adopting a baby, she put two and two together and that's how I came to be with my family!

I think since my parents told me around the time of kindergarten, I was really too young to process what it really meant. They never really followed up with further discussions as I grew older. Because of that, I felt like I had to look at others' experiences and kind of piece together my feelings about it on my own, as opposed to having someone I trust talk through it with me.

I'm absolutely open to talking about my adoption with people! It isn't something you have to feel bad talking to me about. It's not a disease, you don't have to pity me. If you have questions, be bold and ask! I think that being adopted has made me more open and understanding to my students that come from different family backgrounds and made me more aware of how that affects their academic and social lives.

On a logical level, I absolutely wish I knew about medical records and diseases that run in my family, not only just for me but for my future family. Sometimes, I think about reaching out to my biological family to see if I look like them or have similar traits as them.

It doesn't bother me really as much as it used to when people say "real parents," because I know they don't use the word "biological" on a daily basis. The word *real* is just more easily accessible in their brain. But I think that when people call my biological mother my *mom*, I get uncomfortable. "Mom" has this positive connotation and makes people think of a nurturing and loving human that takes care of you, not a crackhead from a trailer park (like my biological mom). But I don't actually get upset at anyone for the way they phrase things or for the words they use - simply because adoption is not a widely-spoken about subject. So many people are naive to the subject and facts, they don't really think about how the adoptee feels.

I always get asked if I want to meet my *real* family, and growing up, that question bothered me. When I was little it would make me scared that if I met my biological mom, she would keep me, and I would never get to see my family again. In high school, it made me angry because I was the age my mom was when she had me. Even as a fourteen-year-old, I couldn't imagine giving up a baby.

But now that I am older, I like answering these questions. I can observe how I have changed over the years, and I can see how I have matured with my answers. I also like how, as an adult, my answer changes every day. Some days, I really want to meet my half-sister that I apparently have, and my grandma. Other days, I want nothing to do with any of them. It's just interesting to me.

In a perfect world, adoptions wouldn't need to happen.

People also ask when I was adopted. I tell them that I went from the hospital that I was born at straight to my adopted family's home, and they usually say something like, "Oh, so they have always been like your real family." That doesn't sit well with me, because I am just as much a part of my family now as I would be if I had been adopted at twelve-years-old. I am the youngest daughter, and my dad told me once when I was really little that I was his favorite youngest daughter (he was sneaky), because he wasn't given a baby, he got to go out and choose me. I know he was being funny and he probably doesn't remember saying that, let alone things that I would remember it, but that has *always* stuck with me.

I have never really thought about adoption jokes until asked for this interview, but I guess I don't like them. Saying that, "You're adopted," as a joke is really more like insulting someone - saying they aren't loved or whatnot. I don't like that at all, that seems to somehow cheapen or make my family less real or loving.

I think it's funny when some people don't know how to talk about adoption with me or if it hurts my feelings, so, at the end, some will say, "That's so cool, I wish I was adopted," to try and (I suppose) make me feel better? That always makes me feel worse.

In a perfect world, adoptions wouldn't need to happen. Everyone would have babies at the appropriate times, would be able to care for them both emotionally and financially, and no one would pass away until that baby was an adult and could take care of themselves. That's not how the world is, and (I assume) in most cases, adoptions can lead to a lot of heartache. The mother has to give up a child she has created herself, the child has to deal with living with a new family and adjusting to their lifestyle and expectations... I just don't like when people say things like that just because they don't know what else to say.

MOLLY

My name is Molly, I am forty-nine, I have been married for twenty-four years. I have two children that were not adopted, and I am the only person in my family that was adopted. I was kept by my birth mother for five and a half months, then foster care, then adopted. When the adoption was finalized, I was one and a half years old. The best part of being adopted to me is that it is who I am. I cannot change it and don't wish to. I have never felt different until this year about being adopted.

This year, I found some of my birth family quite by accident, and it was exciting, but also the first time in my life I have felt weird or awkward about being adopted. I am not dealing with it very well. Adoption had never felt weird or different until recently when I found my birth parent and sibling. That whole thing has been very odd.

I get asked if I want to meet my family. I was once asked, "Don't you want to know them?" I found out some information about them recently. I don't have any curiosity anymore. It is weird that once I had some answers, it seemed to be less important to me to have the information. That once I found it out, I wondered why I felt like I needed to know so badly. I didn't really want to meet them at first, but now I have. I sort of found them on accident online. For me, it was a quick internet search that took me two days. Once I figured it out, I couldn't go back.

My dad passed away about three months after I found and started a relationship with a half-sibling and spoke to my birth mother. I

We just lived life with the fact of my adoption being no big deal. I just embrace it, and it is part of who I am.

have made the choice for now to close the door, because I have been dealing with some weird guilt since my dad passed away and feeling different with my family that I just couldn't be involved with both, if that makes sense.

My parents have always made me feel the same, if not more special, for being adopted. I have two older brothers that were not adopted, and my parents just made it a non-issue by just putting it out there. It has never been an odd thing for me. I don't have any wishes where they (my parents) are concerned. Recently, before my dad passed away, I had the opportunity to tell them both what being adopted to me meant - I told them how much better my life was by being adopted. This was the positive side of finding out about my birth family.

I was born in the same county as I grew up. My birth mother had very few resources, other children, and no connection to my birth father. I think that is why she gave me up. My adopted family was from a different socioeconomic group, and I was provided with many more opportunities and a much easier and stable, loving life. I don't think my age at adoption was that big of a deal. I did move around, so that is part of why it is hard for me to trust people.

Jokes about adoption don't really bother me. I remember kids would say negative stuff like, "You were adopted!" and my parents just told me to say, "Yep, my parents picked me." If the kids were mean, I would add, "And your parents got stuck with you!"

I think people always want to know if you want to find your "real parents," and I always say I know who my "real parents" are. I just don't see my birth parents as relatives. I prefer *birth family, birth parent*, etcetera. I do not like when people say "real" family. I have never been one to hold back on the subject of my adoption. I think that was how my parents presented it. We just lived life with the fact of my adoption being no big deal. I just embrace it, and it is part of who I am.

NADIA

I'm Nadia. I'm twenty-three years old, and I was adopted from Russia. I was in an orphanage, in Nizhny Tagil, Russia, and I was adopted at five months old. My grandmother, Nana, was a teacher in Russia. A friend of hers said that she knew a great Russian baby for Nana to bring to my parent's attention. So, I suppose if they had not talked, I wouldn't have gotten adopted by my family. Especially because my parents were looking at adopting a boy from South Korea. In my immediate family, am the only child, and no one else in my family is adopted.

Earlier this year, I graduated from U-Mass Amherst with a Bachelor of Science degree in Sustainable Food and Farming. I spend most of my free time playing games with my friends, cooking, exploring new places, being with family, or running around with my dog. I'm passionate about changing the food system for the better and helping to save the broken world of agriculture. I hope to someday be remembered for my work and the changes that I hope to be able to make. I currently live in Massachusetts.

The best thing about being adopted for me is having the chance to live the best life possible. I've been able to grow so much into who I am and graduate from college with my dream degree. I'm so grateful that my birth mom chose this path for me because I would have missed out on so much and would not have been blessed with an amazing family and friends who are so dear to me.

The hardest thing for me was not knowing who my birth family was but then being told I had siblings that we knew nothing about. It was an aching hole, which, by lucky chance, got fixed last Summer thanks to a very kind friend who was able to do some research for me. Currently, the hardest part is knowing that my birth mother has passed away and that my sisters really do not know anything about my birth dad. It's not something I've fully come to terms with yet and having a hard time communicating with my birth sisters doesn't help.

I don't know if there was a specific thing that my family has said to me that has helped me understand my adoption. There has always been an open dialogue about it in my family, and they've been supportive and loving through and through. There's nothing really that I wish they knew, other than there are some times that I get really sad and miss my sisters, wish I had more information, and wish so badly that I could get to know my birth mother and thank her and tell her that I love her. I think that my parents know that in their own way.

Being adopted at such a young age was a lucky thing, as it meant that I was able to grow up completely immersed in American culture and the way of life here. For me, it meant that I had no language barrier, no attachment disorders, and that I was able to get the care that I needed for my eyes to be healthy and strong. I got to have so much control over how my life turned out. All I've had to deal with is a learning disability called Nonverbal Learning Disorder, and while it affected me a lot more while I was younger (and it does still affect me), I got the care I needed. I'm really lucky to have such a pain-free story, and that's not something I take for granted, especially after my recent conversations with other adoptees who weren't as fortunate as I was.

I am very open to talking with others about my adoption. I think sharing my story and increasing understanding and awareness of adoption is extremely valuable. It is also something that I want my friends to know about, and I want adoption to never be a topic that is off limits. I have a tattoo representing my adoption, so it is very much something I discuss with people.

I wish that people could understand that every story is different, and that my story is one of unusual luckiness. But, on the flip side to that, I wish people could understand how hard it is to not have that connection to where you came from, to the people who gave you your life and your genetics. How hard it is to have a deceased parent that you'll never know. I also wish people understood how hard the language barrier makes is in talking to my family. Although I've found them, it's not like we're an *insta-family* that automatically clicks. Having blood family who are strangers to you is really hard, sad, and upsetting.

I wish I knew more about the health issues that ran in my family! That is one critical question mark that I will always carry with me, and it is very scary to not know what you could be at-risk for. I wish I knew more about my birth mother and birth father and the family circumstances leading up to my birth as well as what the family dynamic was like growing up and if I was spoken of or thought about.

I don't think that there's much about my hobbies or career that's been influenced by being adopted. It definitely has made me a more open and accepting and loving person, and that's been one reason I connected so well with Unitarian Universalism and why I practice their way of life.

I guess I'm not super-bothered by the phrase "real family," though I do prefer and choose to use the terms *biological/birth family* and *family*. I wish that people would use *biological/birth family* more often, as it helps mark that those are the people that you got your genetics from. I'm not really going to disagree with any specific terms that people use. I don't have a preference of what terms people use when they speak with me.

No jokes about adoption are okay. That crosses the line for me. It's a serious topic and needs to be treated as one. People really offend me when they bring adoption into jokes. My friends know that it is something that I will get mad about, and I rarely get mad about anything.

One of the worst things that someone has said to me relating to adoption was actually a really rude joke, claiming that I had lost most of the sensitivity on my

Having blood family who are strangers to you is really hard, sad, and upsetting.

body because I hadn't been held or touched enough as a baby due to the fact that I was adopted. It really hurt to have them say that. But one of the best comments was my parents saying how lucky they are to have me as their daughter.

I get asked if I know Russian quite often, or if I want to learn. These days, I do get questions about my family, because a lot of my friends know where I am with my search. I also get asked how old I was when I was adopted. There's no questions that I really hate or love, I will answer most of them as long as I am not talking about my adoption all the time. There are some days when I wish I could just forget about it completely and not have this part of who I am.

NAOMI

Hello, I am Naomi, and I was born in Seoul, South Korea. I am a recent graduate of Coe College in Iowa. I was a Psych and Communications double major. I am now a Leadership Consultant for the National Headquarters of Alpha Sigma Alpha, the sorority I was involved in during college.

I think the best thing about being adopted is knowing that you were chosen. My parents do not love me because they have to, but because they put a lot of thought and effort into it, and now there's one less orphan in the world and two happy parents. Sometimes the hardest thing is not looking like my family. I notice it the most in public settings now, and it's a much different experience than when I was younger and obviously with the two adults I walked in with.

There are a lot of racial things that I have become aware of in being different from my family. I am very used to loving people that looking nothing like me, but I know that is not the case for everyone. Now that I am an adult, I can also see how I am treated differently, even though I was raised in the same family. My parents are white, well-dressed people, and they'll get treated a certain way in a store or at a restaurant. They will get waited on hand and foot in a store, but I'll walk in right behind them and get treated differently. I'll get followed to make sure I don't steal anything. It has made me incredibly aware of the racial biases still present today.

The best thing my parents have done to help me not only understand but appreciate my adoption is by celebrating my adoption day. There's a great song by John McCutcheon called "Happy Adoption Day." We play it every year and go out for a nice dinner. It's a simple way to make sure that adoption is something to be celebrated since we wouldn't be a family otherwise.

I had a lot of medical needs as a baby, so I was bypassed from orphanages into a foster home. I am forever grateful for the attention I received from my foster mother, brothers, and family. That period of time can be so crucial for a baby to learn attachment. I was just over a year old when I was adopted. My parents had gone through Holt International Adoption Agency to adopt. The healthcare is not as good in South Korea as it is in the United States which is largely why I was put up for international adoption.

I am grateful to have been adopted as a baby. I hate to say it, but babies are a lot like puppies, in that people want to adopt them young and cute, and become far less interested when they've grown. I have never truly known a life or family outside of what I have now, and that's perfect for me. I might have some distant cousins who are adopted too, but I am the only one I can think of right now.

If you ever wonder if you want to adopt, ask yourself if any child wants to be an orphan.

One thing I wish people knew about adoption, especially for people who were adopted as babies, is that my adopted family *is* my real family. My mom is the one who attended all of my little league soccer games and put bandages on my bruises. My dad is the one who knows my favorite meals and helps me write tough essays. My aunts, uncles, grandparents and numerous cousins are the ones who I have grown up knowing and loving. I always clarify my *birth mother* and my *real mom*. One person gave me the genetics for life, the other has spent years making sure I live a happy life. Blood does not determine family.

I am actually in a huge process right now to find my birth family. My parents have always been okay with me being interested in who gave birth to me. I am also intrigued by the idea of nature versus nurture and would love to know more. I have been searching since I was eighteen, and just recently got a bundle of letters and photos from my birth mother that she has sent me over the years, and so now it is just a matter of making contact.

My least favorite question is if I would ever date or marry one of my cousins. EW! Would you date or marry one of yours?! There's no difference. The worst things I have heard about adoption are from when I was younger. Kids have a hard time wrapping their head around a family concept different than their own, and sometimes they have to work through that through some insensitive comments, none of which come to mind. But I don't have any problems now.

I love jokes about adoption, and I even wrote some of my own. However, I always seem to cringe when other people tease each other about, "You're adopted!" as if it's a bad thing. It's not a bad thing to be adopted. There are lots of good and funny parts about it, but it's never something to be ashamed of.

I will forever be open to talking about adoption to anyone who will listen. There are too few families in the world that are adopting the abundance of children who need homes, so I am a strong advocate for adoption. The last thing I would say is that if you're considering adoption, do it. If you ever wonder if you want to adopt, ask yourself if any child wants to be an orphan.

You'll thank yourself, and they will thank you, too.

Author's Note: Naomi sent in the following update to me.

After five years of searching and twenty-three years of wondering, I finally met my birth mother. Out of the blue, I got an email saying she was flying to New York City on a work trip and wanted to meet my family and me. We rapidly made arrangements to make this possible.

However, for the initial meet up, I flew out alone with my parents coming a couple of days later, so I could do this without worry of how they were feeling.

When it finally came, meeting her was surreal. After years of never looking like someone else, all of the sudden, I was eating New York cheesecake across from the woman who gave birth to me. She's tall and cheerful, just like me. My favorite part, though, was watching her interact with my parents. There was an incredible amount of love and respect shared between them, as well as photos and funny stories of my growing up. So many of my questions were answered, and I got to be in regular contact with my birth brother, whom I absolutely adore.

Now that we've all flown home, it doesn't feel like my family is being shifted or changed, only growing, and that's a blessing I'll strive to be worthy of for the rest of my life.

NEIL

My name is Neil, I'm twenty-three years old, and I was born in St. Petersburg, Russia. The majority of my childhood was spent in the Russian orphanage system. I was in about five to six different orphanages, and I don't remember much about my biological parents, especially not my father. I got adopted when I was twelve by a family in Dallas, Texas. My brother is adopted, too. My dad is a pediatrician and my mother is bookkeeper at his office. I dropped out of high school in twelfth grade after attending some of the best private schools in Dallas.

My relationship with my family was mediocre. My parents and I weren't seeing eye-to-eye. I started to drink and use drugs. I eventually got kicked out of the house and was out on the street, homeless. Eventually, I ended up in a regeneration center called Breaking Free in Davisboro, Georgia. I got my life straight and have had the opportunity to start Breaking Free programs in Costa Rica and Italy.

For me, the best thing about being adopted was a fresh start at life and to have the love and support from a family that loves you. I had a lot of insecurities about myself and the way that I viewed myself. At first, I was very sensitive to the fact that I was adopted and "different" than the rest of the kids I knew. But as I got older, it didn't bother me as much. I sounded different because of my accent. I would act quiet, not because I was shy, but because I didn't want my accent to be made fun of.

Now that I'm older, I would have to say that one of the hardest things growing up was not having a vision for my life and not thinking I could become somebody. As a result, I would rarely apply myself to anything. Fear of rejection.

Since I was twelve when I got adopted, I knew and understood my predicament well. One of the things that my parents would tell me was just how proud they were of me because they understood that what I had gone through and just the whole process of adoption was not easy. Moving to a new country and adapting to everything is not easy and that what I had accomplished was incredible.

My parents did pretty much everything they could to help me to have the best life. I wish they knew just how hard it was for me to connect to people and to feel comfortable in social situations. I wanted to feel comfortable but it was extremely difficult. Even though it's better now, it don't always come easy to me.

I have heard a few Russian jokes here and there, but aside from that I don't feel like being Russian had any negative effects. At first, adoption jokes bothered me and any kind of a remark about the fact that I was adopted bothered me. I feel like you just grow out of being bothered by it. At first, I didn't really like telling people that I was adopted, especially to large groups all at once. Now I don't mind it as much. I feel like it helps people to understand me better. The differences and the similarities.

I feel like all adoptions are different and all adoptees are different. The process is different for everyone based on the difficulty of the life previously lived and the transition into their life ahead. The levels of abuse prior to adoption. It's never easy.

Adoption is hard on both the parent and the child. But when it's all said and done, it will be one of the best things you will do for yourself and the child.

I know that my birth mom was twenty or so when she had me. She passed away when she was in her forties. I would want to know if she had good intentions when she had me. Maybe she just wasn't mature or strong enough to handle a child. Were there other reasons or things that played into my circumstance?

My adopted parents aren't my real parents - *real* meaning birth parents/genetically connected. The term *real* insinuates genetics to me. It doesn't really matter what people say to me, and it doesn't bother me in either way. I view my adoptive parents as my parents.

Personally, I think that people feel awkward or try to be careful asking questions regarding adoption. I can predict their questions and it is usually a brief exchange. Sometimes the questions are about Russia and what the country is like. One of the worst things is when someone made sexual remarks about my parents regarding my adoption.

Adoption is hard on both the parent and the child. But when it's all said and done, it will be one of the best things you will do for yourself and the child. You're giving the child the greatest gift they will ever get. When the child is ready, they will understand that and will thank you for it. Patience is the key.

NINA

Author's Note: The following is a combination of the interview that was sent to everyone and also an article that Nina wrote which previously appeared in the periodical Russian Life *in their March/April 2013 issue.*

My name is Nina, and I am twenty-eight years old.

I was born in St. Petersburg, Russia, and I was adopted with my brother when I was twelve and he was thirteen. Yes, I have my biological brother, Peter, and we were adopted together in 2001. Then, three years later, my parents adopted two more siblings: Maria and Dmitri, who are biological to each other but not to us. All of us came from the same orphanage and knew each other. I am now an assistant coach for a softball team in Plano, Texas. I am a creative person, and I love to make people smile.

The best thing about being adopted is gaining a whole new life. You are adopted into a brand-new family, language, culture, clothes, food, friends, schools, seasons, music, etcetera, that you must learn. You must challenge yourself to become part of them, but also identify who you are and want to be. Being adopted is the greatest thing that has happened to me, and I am able to do anything I want with my life because I have choices.

In Orphanage #2, I didn't have many choices. Food, schools, some clothes, what trips we made, which room I slept in were chosen for me inside the chain-linked fence that we couldn't go outside of. When I first arrived there, I was separated from my brother and taken to a different room, given a bath, and then put to bed because it was nap time. I remember wanting to see Peter, because he was the only family I had at that point. So having the ability to choose is another wonderful thing about being adopted.

The hardest thing for me was FOOD. I am a picky eater. I have been picky since I was born. In the orphanage, if I didn't like something, then I didn't eat it. That meant I would go without food. There were no other options. So, when I came to America, and my parents wanted me to try EVERYTHING at least once, I had a tough time doing it. If I didn't like how it looked, I didn't want to try it. If it didn't taste good, I spit it out. If it had a funny smell to it, of course I didn't want to try it. I still don't eat spicy food, fish, steak, and some vegetables.

You see, before the orphanage, my life was chaotic. My dad was beaten to death when I was young, and my mom was an alcoholic. She was hardly ever there for us, and my oldest brother was in the military for some time. She could not hold a job for more than a day, because she got paid, got drunk, and would not show up to work the next day. I remember waking up in the morning wet, because *she* had peed the bed.

Not many people want to adopt older kids because they think that we have so much baggage, or we can't get over our past, that it's going to be harder to deal with us.

The whole time we were in the orphanage, for about seven years, our mom visited us only once. One time! She came to visit us and took us to the place where we grew up, a home that had almost burned to the ground. This was the "special" outing she had planned for us. What a symbol that house was of our life with her. It was a pile of ashes. The same feeling returned the day the court revoked her parental rights. My eldest brother had to come to sign my brother and me over to be adopted.

Our orphanage director asked if we wanted to be adopted. We both told her "no" several times. I never expected that I would be adopted, but with the way life was in Russia and realizing that no one was going to come get my brother and me, we were ready for a change. To be adopted by people in the United States gave us a chance for a new beginning. After eleven years, I will always remember the life I left behind, but I will never regret making the choice to be adopted, because that was a gift straight from Our Father above.

The best thing that my parents said was, "We want to be your parents." You must understand that because my brother and I were older, we were less likely to be adopted. Not many people want to adopt older kids because they think that we have so much baggage, or we can't get over our past, that it's going to be harder to deal with us. Every child is different and has a different past, same as every parent is different and has a different past. So, knowing that someone does want you in their family helps you not to be helpless in an age group that most people don't want to adopt. I wish my parents knew how much they really mean to me. They really did save us from being orphans our whole life. It has been a long journey from day one, but I wouldn't trade it for anything.

Being an older child had benefits as well. You remember more about your past, you learn differently, you can communicate in different ways. Yes, you have your ups and downs but what teenager doesn't?

I am open to talking about my adoption with other people because I am proud of it. I am proud about what I have accomplished so far in my life, I am proud to tell people I am different and that I have adjusted to a new world. I am proud to give my parents credit for doing something magnificent. Also, I help people see a different point of view. They might have heard about adoption in general or someone they know has adopted, but they have not experienced what it is like from the adoptee's side. People love my story and hearing about what it is like for a child to go through the adoption process. I will continue to share my story.

Adoption is not all rainbows and roses. It is challenging work. It requires work from both sides, the parents and the child. Parents must understand that the child they have adopted or going to adopt is not going to be perfect. He or she is going to be stubborn, have tantrums, fights. But they will also show love, happiness, appreciation in their own way as well. You can't force a child to love you. All you can do is be there for them for whatever they need. Sometimes, that is just to listen without a reply, give a hug or a shoulder to cry on, or just even sit next to each other without doing anything.

Since I was adopted at twelve, I remember many things. There's really nothing I wish I knew because I already know or remember most of it. When I was going to college, I wanted to be a Russian language interpreter. Since I already knew the basics of the language, I thought it was going to be easy for me. Then I started to take harder classes, and I realized that growing up speaking Russian, I basically just knew the slang of Russian and not the proper language.

I agree that I don't like it when people say my birth parents are my "real parents." That has happened to me several times, and I just tell them, "My parents do live around here," or whatever their question was. I don't tell people "my adoptive parents," because they are my *parents*, period. The same goes with my siblings. There is my biological brother, but there are also my two younger siblings who are not biological to me. They are *all* my siblings. I don't separate them into "step" or "adopted" or anything else.

Sometimes the best words for people to understand are the simplest. So, if *real* is better understood than *biological*, then I don't take offense to it. But, in my reply, I will tell them "my biological parents," and continue with my story. I think when I was younger I took more offense to words because other kids had their own perception of me and my adoption. When you get older, you are not as easily offended.

The one question I get asked the most is, "Where are you from?" followed by, "What brought you here?" So I go ahead and tell them my story, the brief version, and they are amazed that I am standing in front of them and what I have been through. My accent is one reason people ask me where I am from. Another question that I love seeing facial expressions to is, "You don't drink?" after I tell them, "I don't drink," and, yes, I am full-blooded Russian.

I honestly haven't heard any adoption jokes. And I can't recall the worst things that someone has said to me. Everything I've heard about adoption has been good things. The best things I've heard are things like, "I'm so glad you were adopted so I could meet you," or "Thank you for sharing your wonderful story," or, "You are a blessing from God."

The one statement I love and hate at the same time is, "I hope my child is just like you." I love hearing that but at the same time hate it, because he or she will not be like me. He or she will not have the same experiences or upbringing as me. He or she will not learn, feel, or communicate just like me.

Being adopted is scary for a child. It took me and my brother about seven years to finally say yes to adoption. Even though we were in the orphanage, we had hope that our biological family is going to come take us back any day. But after so many years of not seeing our biological family, except our oldest brother who came when he could, we knew we had to do something before it was too late. We left our biological family and friends behind. We came to an unknown world and we had to learn EVERYTHING from scratch. It was the best decision we have made and would not trade it for anything.

OLENKA

My name is Olenka. My biological name is Olenka Yagovkin. I was born in 1993 in Russia. I was adopted at seven months old. I was abandoned by my birth mother and eventually sent to an orphanage and children's home until I was adopted. My father didn't even know I existed. I have no memories of Russia, obviously. My adopted folks told me I was adopted at a young age, and I've always wanted to know my biological family.

To me, the best thing about being adopted is knowing I have a better life now than I would have if I had never would have been adopted. Also, I enjoy talking about my heritage to people. The hardest part is not knowing about my homeland that much and not knowing my family tree that well. I never really felt like other kids when I was younger because I am adopted from a foreign country. As far as dealing with it, I'm not sure I have completely dealt with it, to be honest.

Even though I was adopted at a young age, it still affects me...Age doesn't always determine your level of comfort and ability to adjust.

My age didn't influence me since I was adopted so young, and I am the only adopted person in my family. My adopted folks didn't tell me much about being adopted except for the fact that I was. They once told me that Russia is part of my past and should stay there. I wish they knew how that made me feel.

I recently found out where I am from in Russia (Tver), and it is no longer inhabited because there were very few jobs and there was poverty and alcoholism. Both of my biological parents were alcoholics.

For the most part, I am open to talking to people about my adoption, there just may be a few questions that are more sensitive than others. I like for people to know I'm adopted because being adopted from a foreign country makes me feel unique. People don't understand that, even though I was adopted at a young age, it still affects me. I am still only human. Age doesn't always determine your level of comfort and ability to adjust.

To me there are two types of family. My *parents* are my biological family, and my *folks* are my adopted parents. I feel I have to give the woman that carried me for nine months a title even though she abandoned me. I do not like it when people say my adopted parents are my real parents. What does *real parents* even mean?

Recently, I met part of my biological family. I met my sister, her ex-husband, my nephews, and my older brother from my dad's family (my brother and I do not have the same mother). I learned that most of the information on my documents were a lie. But now I know most of the truth, and that has helped me find myself to some extent. Even just having a little information is good enough for me right now.

RACHEL

I am Rachel, and I was born in Berezovsky, Sverdlovsk Oblast in Russia. I was nine weeks premature - weighed only three-and-a-half pounds when I was born. I stayed in the hospital for the first ten months of my life, and then was transferred to a specialized orphanage for the next five months before I was adopted. I'm the only adoptee in the family, but I have three older biological brothers in Russia, as well as three older brothers in America (what a coincidence, haha).

I found my biological family my senior year of high school. I searched for many years, but I wasn't looking in the right place. It has been really interesting getting to know them, and I am very thankful that I have had the chance. It sure has been an emotional rollercoaster.

In January this year, my birth mom finally got her own phone, and now we are able to speak every day (which we do). We message each other every morning and every night. It is just difficult because of the time difference. We have had many deep conversations about everything, and it has allowed me some sense of peace. But I still have many questions that I just can't seem to ask, because I am afraid it will upset her.

I struggle finding positives in my adoption because I look at my family's lives in Russia - and to me, there is no doubt that they could have kept me. Gosh, it really is something I struggle with. But that's when I have to fall back onto God and realize this was His plan.

I feel like my mom (in Russia) and I have this indescribable bond. We talk every once in a while. At the end of a tough week, I was able to talk to her on the phone, and she mentioned that she felt something was truly wrong, but she just did not know what it was. She mentioned that throughout the past week, she had also been having a tough time. I sat there in awe when I heard her say that. Maybe I was reacting to her sadness, or she was reacting to my sadness. The hardest thing for me is missing her, and feeling like she and I are still connected.

Well, my parents always told me that I was adopted, and always shared the story of how they adopted me to basically every new person they met. I guess hearing that story helped. I really wish they knew how much I am struggling with it now. They have no idea, and the thing is, they never even ask how I am doing. It is frustrating, to say the least.

Yes, most definitely I'm open to talking about my adoption. I feel like it is important for many reasons. When adoptees share their stories, they are helping other adoptees to not feel so alone in this journey. It allows them to see that what they are feeling is completely normal and completely acceptable. For me, I wish I had found other adoptees from Russia earlier on. It would have given me such a sense of peace when I most needed it. It certainly does that for me now, but I could have used some earlier.

The adoptee is the most affected person of the triad of birth family, adopted family, and adoptee. They are being separated from their family, their culture, and the life that should have been theirs. I hate when people put the adoptive family or the biological family's emotions and feelings above the adoptee's. To me, that's just not right. The biological family chose to give the child up, and the adoptive family chose to get the child - but that child did not choose *any* of it. They had no say.

Of course, I wish I had all of the medical information, but I really wish I had the life stories of my birth family. I wish I knew what made them happy, or what made them sad, perhaps even scared. I wish I knew their favorite foods, their favorite color, etc. I simply wish I knew them and all they have to offer. Regardless of who they are, or what they've done (including the bad) - they are my family, and I accept them. I love them regardless, and I always will.

For me, I consider my family in Russia my real family, though I never tend to use that term aloud because I would feel guilty. Same goes for using *biological* and *adoptive*. I feel like if I were to call my family in Russia my biological family, then why wouldn't I call my family in America my adoptive family? I just say my family here or my family in Russia.

Sometimes I feel like I would not have been able to survive the past few years without having a relationship with God. During those severe times of struggle, when I wondered why I was even alive, God always seemed to be there with me. He always seemed to be reminding me that everything would be okay, and that I was here for a reason, and this all was happening for a very good reason. Maybe I would not know it then, but certainly, one day I would.

What do I think of adoption jokes? Eh, I guess it doesn't really bother me. I don't let it affect me. But I completely understand why it may hurt someone else who was adopted. I always get asked how old I was, if I remember anything (even if I just told them how old I was when I was adopted, haha).

I also get asked if I have ever been back to visit. I always also get asked if I would rather be here or there - and I hate that question, because people hate my answer - and then they look at me like I am crazy. I would rather be *there*, in Russia. There is no reason that I should have been separated from my mom.

The biological family chose to give the child up, and the adoptive family chose to get the child – but that child did not choose any of it. They had no say.

Sure, maybe life would have been more difficult - but I know for a fact that my heart would not be as broken as is it right now. I simply do not care if I would not have been given a lavish life. To me, I would have happily had to financially struggle in Russia. I guess I just think that love is more important than material items. Material items will only bring you temporary happiness, that is for sure.

I hate when people tell me that just because I was adopted when I was baby, and I can't remember anything, that I should not feel the pain that I do. They think that I should not care so much about my family in Russia. But the separation will always be with me, the heartbreak will always be with me - and there is nothing that can be done to reverse that. It is what it is.

RUSSELL

Hello, I am Russell, a nineteen-year-old freshman at Texas A&M studying biomedical engineering. I was born in Tula, Russia, and I now live in Plano, Texas. I have never really had any hardships surrounding my adoption or thought about it negatively – I was never bothered by the fact that I was adopted. I am where I am, and I am happy. I have always been a positive person, so the best thing about being adopted for me is knowing that I have a second chance at life.

The best thing my parents have said to help me is, "We chose you!" Out of everyone, they picked me and I am very happy. I want my parents to know that I am so grateful. They didn't seek out adoption, and no one else in my family is adopted. My aunt wanted to adopt and she told my parents about it. My parents realized that was an option for them too and got me. The doctor told my parents that I was not going to live past one year old, so I feel like I had a destiny to live. My parents got me as soon as I was cleared by the doctors to go home with them.

I was seventeen months old when they got me and was in an orphanage at the time. I picture my birth city as a very small town. It makes me grateful for where I am. I was so young that my birthplace didn't really affect me because I don't really remember anything. My parents said they knew I would be a good kid because I did not cry at all on the plane ride from Russia to the USA.

I'm absolutely open to talking about my adoption with others! I like talking about it because it is an opportunity for people to learn more. A lot of people don't know about adoption since they haven't experienced it. No one can understand how much you can fully transform someone's life by adopting them. It is a beautiful gift that shouldn't be wasted or squandered. I don't like when people complain about being adopted. There is so much to be grateful for.

I want to know if I had any blood siblings or where my birth family is. I also would love to know medical history. At the doctor's office, I always skip the genetic sections that ask about any diseases from blood relatives.

Adoption has really inspired me to volunteer and help others. I like to volunteer with the Young Men's Service

League. Members of TMSL are involved in serving at soup kitchens, rebuilds, delivering meals, and more. I want to give back as much as I can, and I want to help other people get their second chances.

Honestly, it doesn't bother me when people say "real" family. I just say "my family." They *are* my family - it is not necessary to specify that they are my *adopted* family. I don't know exactly what to call my birth parents. There is my family, and then there are people related to me by blood.

Like other Russian adoptees, I get asked, "Do you speak Russian? Do you know your parents or your heritage?" But I like when people ask me if I like being adopted. This opens up doors for me to share more about it.

Adoption - It is a beautiful gift that shouldn't be wasted or squandered.

I don't get offended by adoption jokes, but it depends on the intentions of the person that made the joke. Maybe my birth dad is a farmer or maybe he is Putin? I don't know! I don't like adoption jokes that make fun of adoption or make adoption seem less. If they are trying to be crude with adoption, it is not funny.

The worst thing I've been asked: "Do you regret being adopted?" I told my fellow classmate that the only regret I have was talking to him. The best: one of my volunteer mentors told me, "You just have so much good. It is amazing

232

that you have such a positive outlook on life." It is sad to me when people don't like being adopted. I don't want people to be bitter towards adoption. A lot of people that want children need to realize that adoption gives children so much hope. I don't want people to pass up adoption - it's not all bad stories.

Adoption connects people. In elementary school, I was going to hang out with my friend Jared. He invited his other friend, who was also named Russell. Jared's mom picked us all up. We were all in the back of his mom's car and the other Russell and I start talking. I asked him where he was from, and he said he was from Russia! It was cool to meet someone with so many similarities. That was the day Jared found out both of his friends named Russell were adopted from Russia.

SOPHIE

Author's Note: I gave Sophie's mother the list of questions and told her to ask whatever she felt comfortable asking her. Here are the responses:

Sophie was adopted from Ethiopia and has four siblings. Of the five total kids, two are biological and three are adopted. She was adopted from an orphanage at ten months of age. She loves to sing, paint and do ballet. She lives in Idaho. Here are the answers to the questions that Sophie, our six-year-old, could answer.

What is the best thing about being adopted?

Having a family.

What is the hardest thing?

Not knowing my tummy mommy or how she looks.

Do you talk about adoption with other people?

I don't really like talking about adoption with people, because sometimes it's just hard and it is private.

What do you wish you knew?

I wish I knew where my Ethiopian family was.

Worst thing that people have said to me about adoption?

Where are your real parents?

TED

My name is Ted, and I was born and adopted sixty years ago in 1956 in upstate New York. I was told I was adopted before I was born. I was in a maternity hospital and stayed there a month "to make sure I was healthy." My adopted parents had waited three and a half years to adopt a baby. I lived in NY until I was twenty-two, then moved to Dallas, Texas. I've always wondered about my birth parents and family history.

I've done DNA testing with three of the DNA testing companies. No relatives closer than possible 2nd cousins on up. I was able to find out some of my heritage, which narrowed it down to UK and northern France and Germany. My adoption was finalized in New York State and, unfortunately, they have one of the most restrictive laws as far as getting access to my original birth certificate and my adoption papers. I had also petitioned the family court I was adopted in, and, despite having what I considered good medical reasons to open my file, it was denied by the family court judge.

The best thing about being adopted to me was having parents and a home to grow up in. I was fortunate and they were very loving and understanding parents. As an adoptee, you're part of two families, but never really fully part of either one.

I just found out within the past year from my eighty-five-year-old aunt that my birth mother (age twenty-seven when I was born) and the birth father had an affair through their working together. My birth father was much older (whatever that means, this was the 1950's, so it could have been five to ten to fifteen years older maybe), and he had a family with kids (which means I have half-siblings out there somewhere). Even though my aunt (and probably my adopted parents) knew that, they *never* told me. She did eventually tell my daughter, when she became aware of my searching for my birth parents.

Another difficulty is that my two kids know their family heritage on their mom's side but not mine. Their nationality on my side was unknown until I did the DNA testing the past couple of years. I don't think I've dealt with the very well. I've always had some insecurity. What has helped the most has been hearing the stories of many other adoptees and hearing about their feelings, how many other adoptees had experienced things I have felt. It's also given me some hope that, maybe someday, I'll be able to get my original birth certificate and possibly find my siblings and birth parents.

My parents always told me they loved me, told me I was "special," I was always part of all their family activities. I wish my parents had asked more questions and gotten more information from the judge when my adoption was finalized… They said he asked them, "What do you want to know?" and they said nothing, assuming I would never want to know my heritage or history or what the situation was. Of course, again, this was 1956, and back then, babies were thought to be "clean slates," and DNA and inherited traits and characteristics weren't in anyone's thoughts.

I was born in a maternity hospital. I was told my adoptive parents brought me home a month later. I don't know what happened during that one month period. Though I was adopted as an infant at one month, the whole adoption process took my adoptive parents about three and a half years.

Aside from being born in a state with closed adoption records, I can't say my birthplace influenced my adoption, especially since I was adopted and had adopted parents waiting when I was born. Upstate NY, outside of Albany, in a small village, was a great place to grow up. I often wonder how close by my birth parents could have been. But it was all I ever knew, being adopted, from my very first memories. I can't remember ever not knowing I was adopted.

Yes, I am open to talking to others about my adoption. It's a big part of my life. Like I said elsewhere, it's helped me to read other people's stories, meet other adoptees and birth parent searchers on social media. I like learning about their experiences and realizing I've had a lot of those same feelings too.

Things I wish I knew that I don't: birth parents, half-siblings, medical history, my original birth certificate, the circumstances of my birth, what my birth mother was told about confidentiality, what was she told, what did she go through...I think of her every day. I can't help but think that every time my birthday comes around, or there's a milestone occurring (high school graduation, college graduation, turning fifty or sixty), that she must think of me.

I was brought up in a Christian (Presbyterian) household, which was actually something my birth mother wanted; she wanted me brought up in a Protestant household, although I was born at a Catholic hospital with an Episcopalian adoption service...maybe she was mad at the Catholic church? I don't know. Birth mother had also named me David, and my adopted parents changed that to Theodore (or Ted, or Coach Ted, as I was known later). Thankfully, my adopted parents both played piano and got me started on piano. Music is a big part of my life and I am either playing instruments or running the folk music coffeehouse I'm involved with. Other than music, I didn't have a lot in common school-wise with my adopted parents. I was good in math and science, so that's why I became an engineer, although, to be honest, I didn't plan a lot for it, it was just,

"You should become an engineer." I've often wondered what my birth parents' careers and aptitudes were.

I agree that I do not like when people say "real family," or "real parents." There's not particularly other terminology I prefer. I use "birth parents" and "adopted parents." I really don't know or have heard that many jokes concerning adoption. People ask if I know my heritage. When talking about my last name, I have to go through the whole explanation that I'm adopted and that's my adopted name, not my original name. And also going through the same thing at doctors' offices, having "unknown" for family history, and having possibly extra tests done because I don't have a history.

Author's Note: Ted emailed me with updates! It has been almost a year since he answered these questions for me, so I was excited to see what he said!

Yes, there has been many updates since I answered these questions.

In February 2017, I found a search angel, a volunteer that helps adoptees analyze their DNA data and who helps build possible family trees, with the purpose of locating birth families and birth parents of adoptees. I had DNA tested in 2015 but did not know what to do with the hundreds of second through sixth cousins that showed up as varying degrees of DNA relatives.

My search angel (Margaret) took in all my information, all my data, everything that relatives told me about my adoption, and our search was underway. In my case, it took about three months to locate my birth mother. A third cousin was found that had an extensive family tree that she shared. We found the common ancestor that me and the third cousin shared, and from that, we were able to fill in the ancestral tree. I learned I had two half-siblings.

Finding my birth families was a life-changing event for me... Every adoptee should be granted the right to see their original birth certificate.

My father's side took a little longer. Searching involves lots of emailing or phone calling and waiting for responses. In my birth dad's side, I ended up writing to my closest DNA relative's account administrator, and through that, I was recognized as looking a lot like the DNA account's great-grandfather, who, turns out, was my biological father. Both birth mom and dad were confirmed with DNA kits that my half-sister and half-brother took on both sides of my birth parents. I have seven half-siblings on my father's side. We were able to communicate through social media, eventually phone calls, then a meeting in their hometown in upstate NY early in November.

I was fortunate in that both families unconditionally accepted me as one of their family members. My birth mom's family didn't acknowledge me at first. Some family members knew of me, some didn't. Most reunions are favorable. We will continue to have contact, and I'll be visiting them again sometime this year. We will keep in contact. Both my half-brother on mom's side and half-sister on dad's side have siblings that have passed away.

Finding my birth families was a life-changing event for me. After years of searching, not having roots or ancestry, something in me changed learning about my bio-parents, knowing the circumstance, suddenly having my nationality confirmed, a family health history, knowing people that looked a lot like me for the very first time. This was also important for my two children, who now know their blood relatives on their dad's side for the first time. I've felt more confident, more empowered having my history, gaining a whole new family. My birth mom passed away in 2014, birth dad in 2005.

Unfortunate that my search didn't find them sooner, I'm sure my birth mom thought of me every day. She kept my birth certificate and adoption papers in her dresser. As well as a picture of my birth father.

Every adoptee should be granted the right to see their original birth certificate when they turn eighteen. Bills are being worked on in the NY legislature so that adoptees that so desire can have access to their records. Other states are opening records, hopefully all (about thirty-three states that have closed records) will allow OBC (Original Birth Certificate) access in the near future.

My adoptive family has been very supportive of my search; they loved seeing pictures of my birth mom and dad. My adopted parents passed away in 2003 and 2005. They were always supportive of my search, and I know they would have been very happy for me if they had known.

TIERNEY

I am a female nineteen-year-old from Ethiopia. At childbirth, my mom passed away due to excessive bleeding. My twin brother and I then were taken to an orphanage by our birth father and uncle. This meant two hours of walking and a bus ride to take us to an orphanage. Our dad couldn't take care of two newborn babies because he had seven other children.

Our birth dad dropped us off at the orphanage, but at that time, they were only accepting children who had both parents deceased. So our dad lied and said he was our uncle with his kids. They took my twin brother and me in. My dad constantly came back to the orphanage to check on us. They began to question it, so he left his babies not knowing what happened to them.

At ten months old, we were adopted into an American family. Luckily, we got to grow up in our Ethiopian culture because our adopted family was working and living in Ethiopia. At eighteen, by God's grace, we got connected with our birth family and, in May 2016, went to meet them for the first time. It was an incredible experience to see my family in great poverty, yet ecstatic joy to see us be reunited. Having two families who equally love me is the best thing about my adoption.

In Ethiopia, it's hard to be adopted because some people don't believe that my white American parents can be my parents. Here in Ethiopia, it's this assumption that I "work" for them; when I'm in public (i.e. the store), I get those stares. I am just patient and when people ask, I explain the situation and it definitely helps.

My parents are great. Through it all, they were open about my adoption. My mom even remembers me, at a young age, asking her why I had this color skin and she had different color skin. She also told me I've asked her what my birth mom's phone number is. The openness and authenticity of my parents' responses spoke volumes. I finally got all my answers this past year when I met my birth family.

My birthplace is a place of extreme, extreme poverty. Being born in the countryside of Ethiopia, there is a lack of medical help. When my mother gave birth, it was natural, and there was no medical services around, and that's a huge contribution to why things happened the way they did.

Adoption consists of grief, too. There are things you work through. It's not all just happy, it comes with challenges. But, on the other hand, I think people need to know that there is so much good and your adopted parents are your parents.

I get offended when people ask, "So do you consider your adopted parents your parents?" I think people need to be careful with their word choices. Once adopted, they are your parents, there's nothing fake about it. But I also say the term *real* when talking with people because they understand that terminology.

I find adoption jokes unnecessary, because it's a serious thing and everyone has a story behind why things are the way they are. Adoptions aren't an easy process, so joking doesn't seem necessary. The worst thing I've been told is probably someone telling me that my parents can't be my parents because of race.

I hate when people ask, "So do you call them mom or dad? How do you know English so well? The best thing is definitely the support and emotion people felt with me when

I met my birth family. I love when people ask, "What do you like about being adopted?"

The openness and authenticity of my parents' responses spoke volumes.

I am glad my twin brother and I were adopted so young, because I recall nothing of my other family and growing up. I would have struggled more if I lived knowing how terrible their living situation is. Adoption is a beautiful thing. For me, it's a reflection of Jesus. I think every believer can support adoption and foster care whether that means they partake in it or just passively support it.

TOMMY

Hi! I'm Tommy, and I'm from Austin, Texas. I was adopted officially at the age of sixteen. I have ten biological siblings and seven through adoption - but I'm the only adopted one in my family. I am a grad of Mississippi College with a degree in History along with Christian Studies. I am currently serving part-time at a church while I search for full-time employment. I feel that the Lord has called me to serve full-time for him in the aspect of preaching and teaching his Word.

My biological family and adoptive family had to all be together in front of a judge. For me, I like that my family made a choice alongside myself to adopt me when I was sixteen. I got to experience the moment that we all had a legal say in my adoption, so it wasn't just my own choice but also theirs as well, and that made me feel so good in knowing that my adopted family had a desire to make me a part of their lives.

I'm the second oldest of seven and, in a lot of ways, the "role model" to my biological siblings. So the hardest thing was leaving my biological family, and I couldn't help but feel guilty and ashamed that I was getting this great opportunity and they were not. This often led to me wanting to prove myself so that I could help my other siblings. I finally dealt with it through understanding that, in my life, God does the work and there is nothing I can do but be myself and stay obedient to what God has laid before me.

Adoption is a need and not just an alternative.

To help me, my parents always said, "We feel God has laid it on our hearts to adopt you." This made me see that God was working in them, and that he was in the orchestration of my adoption. Being sixteen, my age influenced me a lot - it literally turned my trajectory of life around and it helped reshape what the future of my family will look like.

246

Religion has been the biggest, single most pivotal part of my adoption. If it were not for the church, none of the things I do today would be possible. I feel that adoption is a huge part of the testimony God has given to me, so I share to as many as I can. Adoption is a need and not just an alternative. More godly families need to be taking the steps to minister to kids in foster care or orphanages.

I'm cautious about adoption jokes, because I find myself saying similar jokes, so most of the time I let it blow over knowing that most are just being silly.

It's so hard for me to not to see all (biological and adoptive) as family. People want to make distinctions, but to me, I share bonds with both families in different ways. *Real* is so fake to me. Words only give meaning to things that need defining: family is family.

I don't get many questions I love. Sadly, I do get questions about my "real" family and what that was like and how I feel about not being in that situation any more. I wish I knew health risks and just more about what in my family tree ultimately got me here.

The best thing ever said about my adoption was when someone said, "What a game-changer," because it was - I was pulled out of an ugly situation by the grace of God. The question I love most is when people ask how my adoption came to be, and it grants me the chance to share Jesus with them and tell them of how a family was obedient to God's whisper and took me in and made me their own.

TONYA

I am Tonya, and I am adopted from an orphanage in Irbit, Sverdlovskaya Oblast, Russia. I was adopted in the same month I was born (only three years later) in September. Being that I wasn't an infant or a newborn, I experienced some developmental delays, but I worked around them.

My mom is a twin. My aunt adopted from Russia, so then my mom also adopted from Russia. I have four cousins, two of which are adopted. My cousin, who is my mom's twin's daughter, was the one adopted from Russia. My only cousin on my dad's side is adopted from Oklahoma. To me, being adopted is a gift. All my life, I enjoyed telling people I was adopted because I knew it was unique to me. When I was little, I didn't quite get the meaning, but I fully understand and think it is something to be proud of.

I know that there are people out there who have struggled with being adopted and hated all the questions. Struggling with not looking like their parents and all that, but to me, adoption is something that means you aren't growing up in an orphanage. You probably got a better education and a better life (for most).

The hardest thing for me was probably overthinking things. I often thought about my natural parents, mostly as I got older. I tried to tell myself that I didn't want to find them because I knew it would hurt my adoptive parents. I have a tendency to overthink. But I realized that maybe I did want to find them when someone reached out to me and offered to help me. Of course, the process of finding them came with a lot of thoughts. What if they are dead? What if they don't want to talk to me? How the heck do I tell my parents when and if I find them? Do I think I'll be like them?

I dealt with this just by letting it out! I write a lot, mostly fiction, and started to write a fictional piece with a character going through the same thing. I also enjoy photography, and find it sort of therapeutic. I like to think of myself as kind of an active person, always on my feet, so going for walks with the camera was helpful so I could be alone with my thoughts and clear my head. I found my natural mother in March of 2016. My father had died, and I found his side of the family in June of 2016. It's now November of 2016 at the time I'm writing this, and I still talk to my Russian family, and I still haven't told my parents.

Still stuck on how to tell them.

The best thing my parents told me that helped me understand my adoption was the adoption process. They had just recently showed me my documents (which I have read a zillion times), which helped fill in some gaps. I love seeing my parents' videos from their two trips to Russia.

I am pretty open to talking about my adoption with people. I won't usually tell you what happened and why I was put up for adoption unless I know you well. I will answer some other questions about my story because it is important to me.

People ask me if I remember anything, if I know Russian, and if I want to meet my birth family. One of my favorite lines is (if I'm out with one of my parents), "You must look more like your dad," or, "You must look more like your mom." People have told me I kind of look like my dad. My absolute favorite, though, is, "Where do you get the blonde hair from?"

One time, I went to get a facial with my mom. We had the same lady helping us, my mom went first. I could tell the spa lady was looking for similarities between my mom and me. My mom is a short Italian with a tan complexion. The lady said to me, "You have...freckles like your mom..." Later, she said, "You are ticklish like your mom."

I wish people would just have a better understanding of adoption and that it isn't just hard for the parents (birth AND adoptive), but for the adoptee as well. It is still hard even if the child doesn't remember it. A lot goes through one's mind. You can't help but wonder who your parents are or where they are. You constantly think about it. But my *real* family is my family that I grew up with. You're going to tell me that my adoptive family isn't real? Of course, they are real. So I usually use the term *natural*, *birth*, or *biological* instead.

I would just love to meet my birth family and spend some time with them. I like to learn as much as I can about Russian culture and history. I don't really want to know anything about my medical history. I know most people would want to, but I've never had to fill out the medical history part of health forms before - so why start now?

I'm not sure if it's because I was born into a large family or if it is because I was adopted into a small one (I am an only child), but I want a ton of children. Some of my own and some adopted children. I would adopt in a heartbeat. Being a part of an online social media group for Russian Adoptees has really helped me learn and grow.

The hardest thing for me was probably overthinking things.

I don't mind adoption jokes. I haven't really had anyone say anything bad about adoption to me. The worst thing? The worst thing I could think of that anyone *could* say is, "Your parents didn't want you." The best thing I've ever been told came from my adoptive parents, and that is just simply, "I love you."

TRISTAN & AMELIA

Author's Note: Since this interview is from a brother and sister together, it made more sense to leave their responses in the original interview format.

Hello, we are Tristan (age thirty) and Amelia (age twenty-seven) - not biological siblings, but both adopted from South Korea.

What is the best thing about being adopted to you?

Adoption is a good thing that offered us a second chance.

What was the hardest thing for you? And how did you deal with it?

Tristan: We grew up in the South, and we experienced undertones of racism.

Amelia: Having white parents, it was obvious we were adopted and sometimes people were ignorant.

What was the best thing that your parents said to you that helped you understand your adoption? What do you wish they knew?

Tristan: Our parents gave us a lot of books about adoption when we were younger. That helped us know that it was normal.

Were you in an orphanage or foster care?

Orphanage for both.

How old where you when you were adopted?

Tristan: Three months old.

Amelia: Five months – they adopted me when Tristan was four. He still remembers holding me for the first time!

How did your birthplace influence your adoption?

We grew up in a place that was predominantly white, so it was easy for people to know we were adopted. My parents tried to help us understand Korean culture, but we were not really interested.

It is also a challenge getting a driver's license and other documents. Due to our names not being Korean, we often have to provide more than what is required for verification.

What did you wish you knew that you don't?

Amelia: I am happy now, and I have never questioned who my birth parents were - didn't think it was a good idea to find out who they are. I have heard many bad stories.

Tristan: I am not interested in knowing my birth siblings, but I would like to know my medical history. I do not care about learning more about my birth family's mistake.

Has anything in your life like religion, career, or hobbies been influenced by the fact that you were adopted?

Tristan: I felt like I had a debt I needed to pay. I learned about the value of hard work, but I was well-cared for. I wanted to go to West Point, but I was not allowed to go where I wanted because I could not confirm my medical history. This was back over a decade ago. I then decided to work for the government.

Adoption allows us to be more aware of how blessed we are.

What do you think of the term "real family" and is there certain terminology that you wish people would or wouldn't use?

Amelia: My real family is my current family.

Tristan: I see the family that raised me as my real family, not the "family" that left me.

Are there any questions that you always get asked about? What questions do you hate? Which ones do you love?

We do not speak Korean. We *always* get asked about that.

What do you think about jokes about adoption?

Amelia: We do not like adoption jokes. Not a fan.

Tristan: If a stranger says something, there is a problem. If my family jokes about it, then it might be okay.

What is the worst thing someone has said to you about adoption? What is one of the best things?

Amelia: We were the only Asians in our school and kids just do not know what is okay to say. Others were more welcoming.

Tristan: I went to a small private school in the South. In high school, me and a fellow football player who was African American were not allowed to go to certain away-games because of the color of our skin. The school did not want us to get beat up… I felt white growing up. This instance made it obvious how some people are more ignorant than others.

Anything else you want to add about your story or what you want to tell people about what it is like to be adopted?

Adoption allows us to be more aware of how blessed we are.

VANYA

My name is Vanya, I am twenty-eight, and I am from Russia. I was in an orphanage for two years, and I was eight years old when adopted.

My adoptive dad is an artist and had a dream about God holding children. My dad drew what he saw in his dream and felt that the Lord was telling him that these were his kids. He wasn't sure what to do with that, but he told his wife. He got a job at an adoption agency and saw my picture. I was one of the children that he drew from the dream! The rest is history.

It is rewarding to know someone actually came and adopted me and that God has a purpose. My parents fell in love with us and wanted to raise us. They taught us how to be good people with faith, education, and more.

All of my memories from Russia make it hard, but not knowing would be harder. Would I always be questioning the truth? I second-guess my memories sometimes. I ask my siblings to fact-check me.

I was happy in Russia but we had our moments. Why did someone hurt us? Our birth family didn't visit us at the orphanage. They didn't care. But I care for them still.

I had to find balance of how to love all my parents. My adoptive family did not raise me fully, so I wonder if they feel like they would

My life is my life and my adoption is mine.

love me more if they changed my diapers? I had to accept them as my parents while also letting go of the anger I have from my biological parents. It is hard to talk to my birth mom because so much has changed.

I liked the orphanage. Would you rather beg and be broke because your dad beat you up? I went from a horrible situation to a roof over my head with play friends, food, and more. I loved my orphanage.

I remember waiting in the orphanage for my future family with my siblings. I was scared to meet my father because of past abuse. My siblings and I had made choreography to show them. When we met our family, it was amazing. We also got to go to a mall in Russia and tour a little bit of our city with our new family. It was hard when my new family did not speak Russian, so we got really good at charades!

I love Russia still and when I came to America, I had to have a Russian translator help me at school. This really helped me with culture shock. My biological sister and my biological brother were also adopted with me. Then, two years later, my parents went back and got three more Russian children. I also have an autistic sibling adopted from the USA.

I like people to know what adoption is about and what I have been through. Adoption is full of ups and downs, but it's rewarding. You might not ever feel 100% at peace, but that's part of it. It is a blessing that adoption is possible.

I do not like dealing with the Russian stereotype questions. I don't really care one way or the other about adoption jokes. My life is my life and my adoption is mine. Russia was what it was for me. I don't like when people ask me about culture. It has changed, and it was twenty years ago for me.

One time, I was able to talk to my birth mom. She was crying and apologizing. It was hard to hear her upset. I was able to tell her that I love her and forgive her.

XANDER

My name is Xander, and I am from Kansas City, Kansas. I graduated from Baylor in 2016 with a BA in Religion and a minor in Spanish. I am very passionate about my hometown of KC. I am half-African American and half-Mexican American. I currently work at Mission Waco as the assistant youth director. I am a Christian. I am passionate about social justice work. I am going to attend Duke Divinity School in order to earn a Master's of Divinity degree. I am an outgoing person who is fairly confident. I am ambitious. I am a morning person. I am weird at times.

As an adoptee, the best things are the opportunities I have been presented with that I would not have been given otherwise, such as living in a nice suburb, incredible educational opportunities, safer area to grow up in. And it is a great representative of what we as Gentiles should feel like being a part of the body of Christ. The hardest thing to deal with was the constant wondering what my birth parents are like and not being able to spend life with them.

I was two-and-a-half when I was adopted. I think it probably made it easier, being adopted at a young age, to be able to assimilate into my family. Also, my half-brother was adopted. I'm open to talking about this because I know that everyone experiences hardships in their life. I believe that by sharing a part of my story, it helps people start processing their own hardships.

I wish I knew my birth dad, and health risks. I met my birth mom for the first time when she was dying in the hospital. I have experienced my African American heritage in depth, but not my Mexican heritage.

I think my understanding of the world has been influenced by my adoption. I think that my parents' willingness to adopt me and help out me and my birth parents showed me that there is always some way that someone can help out another person. I believe this understanding has influenced my social justice passion and belief that someone can always do more to help another person.

I believe that by sharing a part of my story, it helps people start processing their own hardships.

I tend to say "birth mom and birth dad" and "mom and dad." I could also see why someone who is adopted might say "real family" versus "birth family" due to certain circumstances that might have created bitterness toward a birth family. And like any other insensitive joke, I do not like jokes about adoption.

I wish people could know that not everyone who is adopted lived in an orphanage! I told a girl that I am adopted and she assumed I had lived a miserable life in an orphanage like in the movies. Also, not everyone is thankful to be adopted. Adoption stories are not always these hero stories people try to glamorize it to be. However, adoption definitely needs to become a more popular thing in America. There is a huge need.

ZHENYA

I was in an orphanage for seven years - two in one and five in another. I was adopted three months after my biological mother passed away. I had a good relationship with her, so calling someone else "mom" was somewhat challenging at first. I had to differentiate the terms for myself. I called my biological mom "Mother," and my adoptive mom, "Mom."

I was already almost sixteen when I got adopted, so I understood everything. I wish they understood how challenging it was for me at first because I barely had time to grieve for my biological mother. I got to America a month before my sixteenth birthday. A crazy thing about it is that American law states that international adoptions cannot be done after the child turns sixteen. So it was a close call...

I was already mature, and I personally think it made the transition smoother because I knew what I was getting myself into. I am very open to talking about my adoption because who knows what impact it can make on others? I wish people knew how much responsibility adoption is.

Also, I wish I knew how much I was going to miss Russia. One of my now-sisters was adopted from the same orphanage three years earlier. We are not blood-related, but we were good friends in the orphanage. I'd like to meet my biological father.

I think that both my biological and adopted parents are my real family.

I became a Christian. I already believed in God, but I never read the Bible or went to church. When I got to the USA, my parents took me to church every Sunday, where I learned more about the Bible. I was baptized exactly a year after I got to America. (That was technically my second time to be baptized; first time I was a baby, as per Russian Orthodox beliefs.)

People rarely address my biological parents as my *real* parents, so I personally haven't come in contact with that situation that other adoptees face. However, I think that *both* my biological and adopted parents are my *real* family just because I had a relationship with both and consider them all my real family.

Instead, I get asked all kinds of questions: Do all Russians drink vodka? Do you? Do you still speak Russian? What is the food like in Russia? Do you like USA better or Russia? I don't like this last question because it's like comparing apples and oranges.

When it comes to jokes about adoption, I have a good sense of humor. So as long as it's not meant as an insult, I am okay with it. And honestly, I've never heard any negative comments regarding adoption. Though people don't seem too eager to ask me about it either, because they think it's very personal. But the best thing about being adopted is having a family and people who can be there for you.

ZOEY

My name is Zoey, I'm adopted, and I am fifty-seven years old. I have been a dyslexia therapist in Texas for fifteen years, and before that, I worked with Special Education students for fifteen years. I have taught students with some type of learning difficulty from ages three through high school. I have been married for thirty-three years and have three children and two grandchildren.

The best thing about adoption is knowing that I was wanted and desired. I was not told about being adopted until I was in eighth grade, and I don't know if my parents would have ever told me, but apparently other people knew and the "secret" got out. I was told how that, "no one ever wanted a little girl more than they did." I wish they had told me earlier in life.

Growing up, I didn't look like anyone else in my family. My mother has red hair, blue eyes, and freckles. My dad had dark brown hair and blue eyes. Even my brother, who was also adopted, has brown hair, blue eyes, and freckles. I have blond hair, brown eyes, and olive skin. When we would get together with either side of the family, they would say, "Oh she must look like her father's side," or, "She must look like her mother's people." This was especially hard as I got older. I don't think I really ever dealt with it until I went away to college and discovered that I'm great the way that I am.

I was raised in a small mining town in Arizona (population 1,000), and then I attended college at Baylor University. There were people from all over the country, and what I looked like didn't seem to matter.

My mother and father were married in 1956. They were living in Warren, Ohio. It was the second marriage for my dad. He had three children from his previous marriage. They are over twenty years older than me. My dad was a physician and took a vacation with my mom to Arizona one March. As they drove back, they encountered snow in Ohio. After leaving the sunshine of Arizona, they decided to move. Since my dad was in private practice, he would take care of Medicaid patients.

One of his patients was a lady who was pregnant with her second child from another state. She told my dad that she would be unable to care for another child and asked if he knew of anyone who would want it. So my parents contacted an attorney, who contacted my birth mother. My parents paid for her living expenses and medical care. My dad continued to provide medical care and even delivered me. He once told me that that was the only time he ever spanked me (which it probably was).

Since my dad's office was in a part of their house, my mom was even able to hear my heartbeat before I was born. I was told that my birth mother never officially knew about the arrangement, but my mom suspected she did know. I have no information about my biological father

Anyway, I went home with my parents three days after I was born. The date was January the sixth, which is Epiphany, the celebration of the day the Wise Men brought their gifts to Jesus. So, I've always thought of myself as a gift to my parents from God. The official adoption did not happen until about a year later. There were numerous home visits by the social worker and court even though it was a private adoption.

In the 60s, a stigma still existed that a child would carry the "bad blood" of his or her parents. At least, this was the case with members of my parents' families, so if they hadn't moved away from family in Ohio, I probably wouldn't have been adopted (at least by them). I wish I knew my heritage, any siblings, or any major health risks. I always have to tell doctors that I don't know my family history, I wish they would put a box to check as "unknown."

When you're adopted, you know that you were wanted and loved, and that's probably the best.

My brother, who was also adopted, was born in August 1960. I was born in January 1960. His adoption was more commonly known by the people in our small town. For several years, my parents even celebrated his birthday in October so we would seem to be nine months apart. Appearances were everything. My mother even once told me that his mother was very young and didn't take care of herself like mine did.

My brother did not have as fulfilling of a life as I did, even though we were raised by the same parents. He died when he was twenty-three and was into drugs. The death was not drug-related, but sometimes someone would say, "Oh, he's adopted..." as if that was a reason or excuse for his bad behavior or poor choices. I personally think jokes about adoption are in very bad taste. . .

Still, I am open to talking about my adoption. What I wish other people could understand about adoption is that it is the best for both involved parties. There are many childless couples who just want a child of their own, but are unable to. I think of them as my family, and I call my biological parents "birth parents." I'm not too fond of the term *real family* because the only family I've ever known are the ones that raised me. The question of my adoption is not known to everyone and because at my age, it's not a big deal.

I'm not sure if my mother-in-law fully embraces it (adoption). She often asks if I know anything about "my people" (birth family). When I tell her about my parents' heritages, she will say, "Not them (adopted family), your 'real people.'" Like I said, the only "real" people are the people who raised me.

When you're adopted, you know that you were wanted and loved, and that's probably the best. I have never dwelt on the reasons why I was put up for adoption, I've always just accepted it as a fact.

FINAL THOUGHTS

Recently, I got to attend my first adoption court finalization as part of my schooling for my Master's in Social Work. I was standing in the courthouse and a million thoughts were going through my head about how amazing and emotional this whole process is. The foster parents and their foster child walked up to the judge. The judge asked the foster parents, "Is this adoption in the best interest of the child?"

The child screamed, "Yes!" So precious. So thankful. There was not a dry eye in the courthouse and the smile on that seemingly stern judge's face was a sight to see. They walked in as a foster family, and out as a forever family.

Also not long ago, I visited my adoption agency. There was an opportunity to go to a training there as part of my field experience for school. They were kind enough to give me a tour of the facility. I even met a women who has been working with adoption for over twenty-five years. And guess what? She even worked on *my* family's adoption case! She told me that she enjoyed matching families with babies and seeing how families came together. She said that she remembered meeting my parents and talking with them during the adoption process. At that, I just burst into tears and cried telling her how much I appreciated her, adoption agencies, Jesus, and life.

This writing process was very cathartic for me and most of the other adoptees in this book as well. If you're an adoptee reading this, I would encourage you to write out your thoughts, too! Do not be afraid to talk about your adoption; it impacts every adoptee differently because we are all different people with individual stories.

For those of you who are not adoptees, I hope that you now have a better grasp of what adoption is like and why it can have such an impact. While not all perspectives of all kinds of adoptions were represented, this book is meant to serve as part of a greater and ongoing dialogue about adoption. The conversation doesn't end on the last page, so I would love to hear your thoughts, too.

Is there a certain adoptee that you connected with? How will you use what you read to be a better influence in the world around you? Adoption should not be an excuse to act like a victim or act like you are better than someone else. But adoption *does* have lasting effects throughout the adoptee's life, and I know that everyone can learn something from adoption. I hope that you wake up thankful for at least an ounce of your life's circumstances.

There is a reason people are drawn to stories of adoption: the processes, the outcomes, the backstories. It looks a little different now than even when I was young as policies continue to change in the United States and in other nations. Nowadays, adoptions can happen through private adoption, foster-to-adopt programs, and international adoptions. But one thing that hasn't changed is the immense amount of loss combined with indescribable hope.

How beautiful, emotional, and crazy life can be through adopted eyes. I would know.

ADOPTEE STORY INDEX

Due to the breadth and scope of different adoption stories represented in this book, we wanted to provide readers with an index to help them quickly return to stories representative of various popular topics concerning adoption.

DOMESTIC, PRIVATE

DOMESTIC, FOSTER CARE

DOMESTIC, OPEN ADOPTION

ELIZA

HEATHER

INTERNATIONAL, RUSSIA

ALICIA

ALINA

ALLIE

ANDREA

ELIANA

ERICA

ERIN

GINNY

JIMMY

KATHRYN

KENDRA

LARA

LAUREN

NADIA

NEIL

NINA

OLENKA

RACHEL

RUSSELL

TONYA

VANYA

ZHENYA

INTERNATIONAL, CHINA

EMERY

HAILEY

INTERNATIONAL, ETHIOPIA

CHRIS

SOPHIE

INTERNATIONAL, SOUTH KOREA

NAOMI

TRISTAN & AMELIA

FOUND BIRTH FAMILY

AMY	ANDREA
BRYNLEE	CARISSA
CHARITY	GINNY
HEATHER	JAKE
KARA	MIKE
MOLLY	NADIA
NAOMI	OLENKA
TED	TIERNEY
TONYA	XANDER

OUTSIDE OF THE UNITED STATES

ARJUN	ERIN
TIERNEY	

KID PERSPECTIVES

CHRIS	SOPHIE

MATURE PERSPECTIVES

CHARITY	MIKE
TED	ZOEY

SINGLE-PARENT HOME PERSPECTIVE

ALICIA

RECOMMENDED RESOURCES

While we hope that this book is a treasured resource for you, we also recommend you check out the following resources concerning adoption and related topics:

Books for Grown-Ups

- *The Connected Child*, by Dr. Karyn B. Purvis and David R. Cross
- *The Whole-Brain Child*, by Daniel J. Siegel and Tina Payne Bryson
- *Twenty Things Adopted Kids Wish Their Adoptive Parents Knew*, by Sherrie Eldridge

Books for Kids

- *Rosie's Family: An Adoption Story*, by Lori Rose
- *A Mother For Choco*, by Keiko Kasza
- *Baby Owl Lost Her Whoo*, by Cindy R. Lee

Films for Grown-Ups

- *Short Term 12* (2013), directed by Destin Cretton, starring Brie Larson and John Gallagher, Jr.; rated R for language, some mild sensuality, and thematic material.
- *Lion* (2016), directed by Garth Davis, starring Dev Patel, Rooney Mara, and Nicole Kidman; rated PG-13 for language, some mild sensuality, and thematic material.
- *Juno* (2007), directed by Jason Reitman, starring Ellen Page, Michael Cera, Jennifer Garner, and Jason Bateman; rated PG-13 for language, some sensuality involving teenagers, and thematic material.

Films for Kids

- *Tarzan* (1999), directed by Chris Buck and Kevin Lima; rated G.
- *Lilo & Stitch* (2002), directed by Chris Sanders; rated G.
- *Kung Fu Panda 2* (2011), directed by Jennifer Yuh Nelson; rated PG for fantasy-style cartoon violence.

Online/Other

Empowered to Connect, empoweredtoconnect.org
Overcoming Odds, overcomingodds.today
Transfiguring Adoption, transfiguringadoption.com

ABOUT THE AUTHOR

Elena Svetlana Hall is a proud alumni of Baylor University working on her Master's degree in Social Work. Her passion for adoption advocacy stems from her faith and family. Those who know her best know that she talks very fast and loves ice cream, singing, dancing, white rice, spending time with friends and families, and all the gluten things. But please keep cilantro far away.

Made in the USA
Lexington, KY
23 March 2019